730.9

Blairsville Junior High School
Blairsville, Pennsylvania

YOUNG PEOPLE'S STORY OF
OUR HERITAGE

YOUNG PEOPLE'S
STORY OF
OUR HERITAGE

———————————◆———————————

SCULPTURE

by

V. M. HILLYER and E. G. HUEY

New Edition Designed and Revised by Childrens Press, Chicago

Consultants

Ruth Esserman, Chairman, Art Department
Highland Park High School, Highland Park, Illinois

Everett Saunders, Art Lecturer, Northwestern University
Art Consultant, Wilmette School System, Wilmette, Illinois

Meredith Press, New York

3646

730.9
Hil

Illustrations in the order in which they appear

Library of Congress Catalog Card Number: 66-11325

Copyright © 1966 by Meredith Publishing Company. Originally published under the title of *A Child's History of Art* by V. M. Hillyer and Edward G. Huey. Copyright, 1933, by D. Appleton-Century Company, Inc. Copyright, 1951 by Appleton-Century-Crofts, Inc. Copyright, 1961 by Mercantile Safe Deposit and Trust Co. All rights reserved. Printed in the U.S.A. Published simultaneously in Canada.

Contents

Acknowledgments

Cover, top: **Chinese glazed pottery horse, T'ang Dynasty.**
Courtesy of The Art Institute of Chicago, Gift of Russell Tyson

Cover, bottom: William Bowie, sculptor. **From The Sculpture Studio, New York.**
Hedrich-Blessing Photograph

page 2: Michelangelo, **The Pietà.** St. Peter's, Rome.
Alinari-Art Reference Bureau

Frontis: Ghiberti, **Gates of Paradise.** Baptistery, Florence.
Alinari-Art Reference Bureau

opposite: **Guardian Lion from the tomb of King Tutankhamen, son-in-law of Akhenaten.**
Historical Pictures Service, Chicago

Designed by John Hollis

Edited by Joan Downing Soltz

SCULPTURE

Marburg-Art Reference Bureau

Egyptian Relief Sculpture

Most of you have, at one time or another, made a sculpture. Maybe you have rolled a piece of soft clay into a long thin roll and coiled it to form a basket. Maybe you have made a figure of an animal from soft clay or soap or wood, or shaped a piece of aluminum tubing or copper wire into an interesting design. There are many kinds of sculpture, and most of us have tried to do one kind or another. Very few of us have gone on to become great sculptors.

Men have made sculpture ever since the world was young. But at first the sculpture that men made was very little different from drawing. The artist first drew his picture on something flat, than he carved the lines deeper so that, if it were outside, the rain would not wash the drawing away and the weather would not wear it down. This kind of drawing or sculpture is called *sunken relief*.

After that, sculptors rounded the edges of the figures they had carved and cut away the background so that the figures stood up a little above the background. This is called *low relief* or *bas relief* (spelled bas but pronounced bah), which mean the same thing. You may have a bas relief in your pocket. A penny, nickel, dime, or any other coin that has figures on it is done in bas relief.

Then sculptors began to round the figure still more and cut away more of the background so that the figure stood out still more. This kind of sculpture is called *high relief* or *half round*, for the figures were halfway out of the background.

Later, sculptors cut away the background entirely, so that the figure stood out all by itself. This is called *full round*—you can go "round" it. You will see such pieces of sculpture in parks, squares, and museums.

Long, long ago Egyptian artists carved pictures in sunken relief on the walls of their great buildings. Such figures are cut on the gates of a great temple in Egypt.

Great Temple Gates. Pylon from the South. Horus Temple, Edfu.

Egyptian State Tourist Administration. Photo by C. Zachary.

Egyptian State Tourist Administration. Photo by C. Zachary.

above left: Bas relief from the Temple of Luxor.

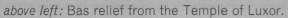

above right: High relief statue of Rameses II at the Grand Temple at Abou Simbel.

Some figures are sitting and some are standing. All of them may look peculiar to you. Can you tell why? Two things about these carved Egyptian pictures or sunken reliefs may seem very strange to you. I wonder if you can see what these two peculiar things are.

Here is the first thing: the feet are stepping directly sideways and the faces are all turned sideways too, but the shoulders are front view. Now, of course, no one really walks that way, with head and feet sideways and shoulders front view. So the first strange thing is that the figures are twisted.

The second thing is the eye. What you see are the side faces— the profiles—not the front faces; yet the eyes are the shape of eyes when they are seen from the front, not as seen from the side. All Egyptian reliefs had the same peculiar shaped eyes, also the same twisted bodies. Shoulders and eyes are front view, while everything else—hips, legs, and feet—are sideways.

The Egyptian kings and queens wore crowns that had special meanings. The queen in the Great Temple Gates relief is shown with a crown that looks like a bird called a vulture; above the vulture is a moon between two horns. The king's crown is called a pschent (p-skhent').

These figures are all sunken relief. The next kind of relief is called low relief or bas relief, as we have mentioned.

One of our illustrations shows a bas relief from the Temple of Luxor. The peculiar designs on the side of the picture are a kind of picture writing called *hieroglyphics*.

At the Temple at Abou Simbel, in Egypt there are four huge figures that are carved in high relief. They are almost cut away from the background, but not quite. These figures are colossal, which means gigantic, huge, or mammoth. A real man standing beside one, wouldn't reach halfway to the knee. The Egyptians made many giant figures. These giant figures at Abou Simbel are seated in a very stiff position, sitting bolt upright, with both feet flat on the ground and both hands flat on the knees. They are all figures of the same king, Rameses II, called Rameses the Great, for he was one of the greatest of all the Egyptian kings, though also one of the most cruel.

Rameses II was the Pharaoh who ordered all the Israelite babies killed, and it was his daughter who found the baby Moses in the bulrushes and saved his life. Rameses built many temples and statues of himself. He had the Temple at Abou Simbel cut out of the rocky cliff, and had the huge statues of himself carved on the front.

Colossal high relief figures of Rameses II at the Grand Temple at Abou Simbel.

Trans World Airlines, Inc.

Trans World Airlines, Inc.

Egyptian State Tourist Administration. Photo by C. Zachary.

Colossal and Miniature Sculpture of Egypt

Egyptian sculpture in the full round was usually giant size, as tall as a house, or the other extreme—tiny statues only an inch or so high. The statues of their kings and important people, the Egyptian sculptors usually made in giant size—colossal. They thought a statue the size of an ordinary man or woman was not nearly big enough for a king or a queen.

The biggest statue in the world is *The Great Sphinx*, which is near the three great pyramids. It is a huge lion with a king's head. The Egyptians often combined men and animals in this way, but more often they put an animal's head on a man's body.

The Great Sphinx was supposed to be the God of the Morning, and so he faces east—he is always facing the rising sun and gazing at it unblinkingly, as he has done each morning for thousands of years. His nose is as tall as a man. The triangular pieces at the sides of his head are part of a peculiar hood.

There are many more sphinxes in Egypt, but the others are much smaller than *The Great Sphinx*. These smaller sphinxes usually were arranged, with many of them in a double row, to form an avenue leading up to some temple.

Farther up the Nile, there are two colossal seated figures sitting on thrones side by side, gazing out over the plain. They are called *The Colossi*, because of their colossal size. Each is made out of a single stone. They are weather-beaten and broken, but you do not need much imagination to be able to tell what they once were. The two statues are of the same Egyptian king. These two also face the sun as it rises in the east. One of them is called *The Vocal Memnon*—that is, the singing or sounding Memnon—though Memnon was not the king's name. His name was Amenhotep. We know the names of very few of the old sculptors who made the statues, but we do know the name of the sculptor who made these statues of Amenhotep, for he had the same name as the king. Perhaps he was a slave.

It has been said that *The Vocal Memnon* at one time gave forth sounds, perhaps like the tones of a great organ, when

British Overseas Airways Corporation

Colossal statue of Rameses II in the full round, Cairo.

---

upper left: **The Great Sphinx**, near Cairo.

---

lower left: **The Colossi of Memnon** at Luxor.

Blairsville Junior High School
Blairsville, Pennsylvania

the sun rose—a hymn to a new day—though *The Vocal Memnon* apparently did not sing every morning or even every year. When it did sing, it was supposed to be a sign of something—an omen people called it—but an omen of what, no one knows. It is believed that about the time of Christ it was upset by an earthquake and that when it was replaced, it ceased its morning song. It has not sung for nearly two thousand years; some people doubt that it ever did sing, though people even at the time of Christ traveled long distances just to hear it sing and were disappointed if it didn't. Many who did hear it, however, have carved on the base their names and the dates when they did hear it. So there seems to be little doubt that it did sing once upon a time. Some scientists think the sun's rays striking the cold stone in the morning wrought some change that made the sound. It is one of the many mysteries of Egypt.

It is strange that one of the oldest pieces of sculpture in the world is made of wood—strange because wood of course does not usually last as long as stone. Strange, too, that it is not the statue of a king or a queen or a god, for that is what the Egyptians usually made.

This piece of sculpture is the figure of *Ka-aper*, a rather small, fat, bald-headed man carrying a tall staff, or walking stick. The statue is small, smaller than a real man, perhaps to show that he was not a king. Some people think he is a priest; others say he is a schoolmaster or the chief of a tribe. Still others say no, he looks like the boss of a gang of workmen, possibly one of the gangs that worked on *The Great Pyramid*. So you can take your choice, for no one knows just what he was. The statue is in the great museum at Cairo, the capital of Egypt. Though it was made so long ago, it looks much more natural and lifelike than later Egyptian sculpture—very much like a real person. It is said that even the old Egyptians thought it so natural that they chained its feet to keep it from walking off!

Another figure made about the same time is of a seated man who is holding a writing tablet on his lap. This statue is of stone. The man was a professional writer—that is, one of the few men who knew how to write and who made a business of writing for those who did not know how. Such a person was called a scribe. He was a kind of secretary who took dictation. Even kings and queens could not write and had to have scribes write for them. This figure is now in the Louvre in Paris.

Often Egyptian sculptors went to the other extreme and made statuettes, some only a few inches high, of their kings and queens, their gods and goddesses, and their sacred animals.

Egyptian State Tourist Administration. Photo by C. Zachary.

Ka-aper. One of the statues at the Egyptian Museum, Cairo.

Alinari-Art Reference Bureau

Seated Scribe. Louvre, Paris.

Art Reference Bureau

A scarab, (front).
British Museum, London.

Art Reference Bureau

A scarab, (back)
British Museum, London.

Most of these miniature statues were cut out of the hardest kinds of stone—stone that would turn the edge of our modern tools. We suspect that they must have been cut with flint tools instead of steel tools—as today a diamond, the hardest of all stones, must be cut with another diamond or shaped by being rubbed with diamond dust.

The beetle, called a scarab, was sacred in Egypt, and numberless scarabs made of clay and stone were made to be worn on a chain, as necklaces. A scarab worn in this way was thought to be a charm for the wearer. Scarab charms are so popular today that they are manufactured in great quantities and sold to travelers as real antiques.

19

Historical Pictures Service, Chicago

Limestone bust of Queen
Nephertiti, wife of Akhenaten.
Berlin Museum, Dahlem.

Historical Pictures Service, Chicago

UAR Information Center. Embassy of the United Arab Republic.

above: Golden mask of King Tutankhamen. Egyptian Museum, Cairo.

left: Gold coffin of King Tutankhamen, son-in-law of Akhenaten. Egyptian Museum, Cairo.

Assyrian cherub. Winged bull, a guardian of the palace gate, alabaster. From the Palace of Ashur-nasir-apal II (885-860) at Kalhu, modern Nimrud.

The Metropolitan Museum of Art, Gift of John D. Rockefeller, Jr., 1932.

Assyrian Alabaster

Can you speak Assyrian? What's that? Of course not? But you know one Assyrian word, I'm sure, even though you may not know about the country. Assyria is about a thousand miles to the east of Egypt. Like Egypt, Assyria is an ancient country. The Assyrian word I think you know is *cherub*.

We call an angel head with wings a cherub. Sometimes we call a sweet baby a cherub. But an Assyrian cherub is neither. It is an animal, either a lion or a bull, with a man's head and large wings. In Assyria cherubs used to be cut from alabaster, a kind of stone, usually white, that was softer than most of the stone the Egyptians had.

The Egyptian sphinx was a man-headed lion lying down. The Assyrian cherub was a man-headed bull standing up. Look at the picture of the Assyrian cherub. Notice its man's head—how carefully and tightly the hair and beard are curled. Even the end of the cherub's tail is curled.

This cherub has *five* legs! The sculptors knew, of course, that a bull had only four legs, but they made him with five legs so that a person looking at him from the front would see two legs together as if he were standing still, but when looking at him from the side would see the animal walking.

The next piece of Assyrian sculpture is in low relief. Notice what muscles these men have—how different from the Egyptian men, who were slender, with no muscles showing. The Assyrians thought that beauty was strength—that one must be strong to be beautiful—so they showed their kings with big bulging muscles.

The Assyrians believed also that hair was a sign of strength, and that no real man who could grow a beard would have a smooth face like a woman. You have probably heard the story of Samson, whose great strength supposedly was due to his long hair and who became weak when it was cut off. The king in this relief has long hair and a beard tightly curled like ropes, but the servant has no beard. That was because servants were not supposed to be as strong or manly as kings, and so were not permitted to wear beards.

Notice that the eyes are drawn in the same way the Egyptian eyes are drawn—front eyes in profiles. Assyrian men had more clothing on than the Egyptian men—shawls or skirts with tassels that came to their ankles—and they wore half sandals. They were not altogether barefooted.

The two things the Assyrian kings liked to do best—their two chief sports—were killing animals and killing people in battle, so most of their reliefs show them doing these things.

The best things the Assyrian artists made were figures of animals. They made much more lifelike animal sculptures than those of the Egyptians. In many reliefs the horses are fine, spirited steeds with tightly curled manes and tails.

The Assyrians also made tiny reliefs on the curved surfaces of spool-shaped pieces of clay or stone. A small axle was put through the spool hole and the spool then became a tiny rolling pin that could be rolled over any soft surface such as mud or wax to leave a flat imprint of the picture on the spool sides.

We think they used these seals to sign their writings. They did not write on paper, for they had no paper. They wrote on mud bricks before the bricks were dried and they stamped their seal at the end instead of signing their names.

These Assyrian sculptures have been dug up from the ruins of their old cities, carried away, and placed in museums, so that if you want to see them, you must go to the British Museum in London, the Louvre in Paris, the Metropolitan Museum of Art in New York, or to other great museums.

We don't know much more about Assyrian sculpture dug up from the ruins of once-great cities and carried to the museums of Europe and America. Not much is left to tell the tale of the proud, powerful, and cruel tyrants who ruled over millions of people—monarchs and their subjects all dead for thousands of years.

Nelson Gallery-Atkins Museum (Nelson Fund), Kansas City, Missouri   Historical Pictures Service, Chicago

far left: Assyrian low relief from Nimrud. 9th century B.C.

left: Assyrian alabaster high relief of the hero Gilgamesh holding a lion cub, from Khorsabad, Iraq. Paris, Louvre.

below: Assyrian lion hunt, King Ashur-bani-pal. British Museum, London.

Reproduced by courtesy of the Trustees of the British Museum

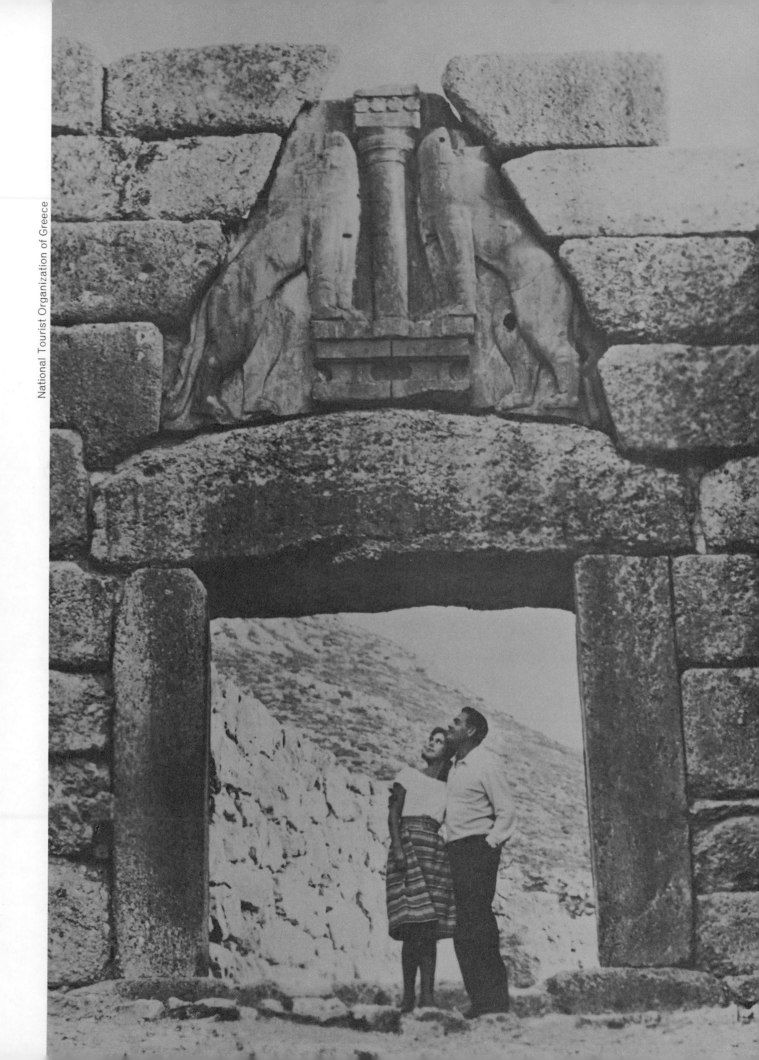

National Tourist Organization of Greece

Early Greek Marbles

Greece is a little bit of a country in the Mediterranean Sea. The ancient Greeks who lived there and the modern Greeks who live there now are very different.

The ancient Greeks believed in many gods and goddesses and heroes, and made up fanciful stories about them—we call it mythology. The Greeks also made beautiful statues of their gods as they supposed the gods looked and acted, and no one since has been able to make sculpture as beautiful.

The Egyptians usually made their statues of granite, which was very hard. The Assyrians made theirs of alabaster, which was very soft. But the Greeks made theirs of marble, which was just right. One reason they were able to make such beautiful statues was that they had such beautiful marble to make them of—just the right material.

In Greece there were several places—quarries—where the finest marble in the world was found. One was a mountain called Pentelicus, another an island called Paros. There is still plenty of marble from Pentelicus and Paros, but there is no one now living who can make it into such sculpture as these Greeks who lived two thousand years ago. It takes more than good marble to make a good statue.

But the Greeks did not make beautiful statues from the beginning. One of the oldest pieces of Greek sculpture we have is of two lions over a stone gateway at a place called Mycenae. The heads are missing from these lions, but even with the heads they once had, they could not have been any finer than some of the Assyrian lions cut in alabaster.

One of the next oldest pieces of Greek sculpture looks almost like something a child might have done, but that is to be expected, for it was made when Greece was a child. It tells a story, however, very well—the Greeks' story of Perseus and Medusa.

The Lion Gate, Mycenae, Greece.

Alinari-Art Reference Bureau

According to Greek mythology, Medusa was a beautiful girl who committed a terrible sin against the goddess of wisdom, whose name was Athene. Athene, to punish Medusa, turned her into a horrible-looking creature and turned the locks of her hair into snakes that writhed and twisted about her face. So terrible was Medusa's face that anyone who looked at her was turned into stone. A young hero named Perseus was dared by an enemy of his to cut off Medusa's horrible head. The goddess Athene, who was a friend of Perseus, led him to Medusa. When he came to the place where Medusa lay asleep, he looked away and cut off her head with one stroke. As he did this, out sprang a winged horse called Pegasus.

In the picture, Perseus is shown cutting off Medusa's head as he looks away. Medusa clasps Pegasus in her arms. Athene, on the other side, is facing front, but her foot is twisted sideways so that it will fit into the picture. Medusa's right leg is longer than the left, for the left leg is very short from the knee up. If you can imagine how she would have looked if she had stood up, then you can see better how much shorter one leg is than the other.

The Lion Gateway and *Perseus* are both in high relief. A statue in the full round that was made later is called *The Apollo of Tenea.* Apollo was the Greek sun god and was supposed to be the handsomest of all the gods, but this statue of him may not make you think he is very good-looking.

The Greeks of those days thought the human body the most beautiful thing in the world. They tried to make their own bodies beautiful by physical training—sports, exercises, and healthful living—and they made statues of their most famous athletes.

This statue probably is not Apollo at all, but just the figure of an athlete—a runner or a jumper. He is not beefy like the Assyrians or skinny like the Egyptians; the face has a peculiar expression, the hair is primly crimped, and the eyes seem to bulge. This is one of the first statues we have that seems to be smiling.

This early or *archaic* sculpture, as it is called, is interesting, but from this period on the Greek statues are not only interesting but really beautiful.

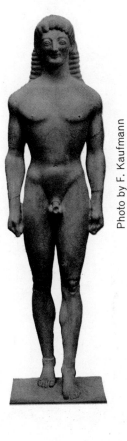

Photo by F. Kaufmann

left: Metope of **Perseus and Medusa.** Museo Civico, Palermo.

right: **Apollo of Tenea.** Staatliche Antikensammlungen, Munich.

29

Alinari-Art Reference Bureau

Classical Greek Sculpture

When I used to speak at school assemblies, I stood like an Egyptian statue of Rameses—hands straight down at my sides and feet close together, flat on the floor.

"Stiff as a poker," my teacher used to say. "Can't you take a more natural position? Put one foot behind the other!"

So I stood like the wooden statue of *Ka-aper*, but still with both feet flat on the floor. That was the best that I could do to be natural, and that seemed the best that sculptors were able to do with their standing statues until a Greek named Polyclitus (Pol-ly-cly′tus) came along. Polyclitus made a statue of an athlete carrying a spear over his shoulder. It was the first time a statue had been made in an easy, natural standing position, with the weight resting on one leg, one foot behind the other and *not* flat on the ground.

The Greeks called this statue of *The Spear Bearer* the perfectly proportioned man, the ideal figure, and other sculptors used it as a pattern and copied its proportions in the statues they made. Live athletes exercised to try to make their own chests and legs and arms the same size as those of *The Spear Bearer!*

Polyclitus also made a statue of a woman athlete. It was called *The Amazon*. The Amazons were supposed to be a tribe of warlike women who fought men in battle and even in duels.

Other sculptors admired these two statues and made copies of them in marble. It is fortunate for us that they did so, for all we have now are the copies. The ones that Polyclitus himself made have disappeared and no trace of them is left. What became of them no one knows.

Polyclitus made his statues of a metal called bronze. The first metal ever discovered was not gold or silver or iron, but copper. Then tin was found; and tin and copper combined made bronze. So bronze is not a pure metal. It is a combina-

The Spear Bearer. Museo Nazionale, Naples.

Alinari-Art Reference Bureau

tion of copper and tin. Bronze lasts if kept dry, but when it is exposed to the weather or dampness, it is gradually eaten away. This metal could be worked so well that the Greeks loved to make statues and other things of it. It does not rust like iron, it is not expensive like gold or silver, and as it grows older it turns a rich brown or greenish color and in the course of time acquires a coating called a *patina*.

I have an ancient lamp made of bronze with a beautiful patina that it took perhaps two thousand years to acquire. Some people try to imitate the real patina by treating bronze with acid, but only nature and time can make the real patina.

Myron, another Greek sculptor, was a friend of Polyclitus. Myron went further than Polyclitus in giving naturalness and action to his figures. One of his statues was called *The Discus Thrower*. The discus was a heavy, flat, circular plate—a disk—and discus throwing was a sport in which the object was to see how far the discus could be hurled. The discus had to be hurled underhanded, as in bowling, not overhanded. It wasn't rolled along the ground, but was hurled into the air.

The Discus Thrower is shown just at the moment before the discus is to be hurled from his hand. Notice that the toes of the front foot grip the ground and those of the rear foot are being drawn along the ground to balance the body. The discus weighed between three and nine pounds and the record throw was less than a hundred feet, which may not seem very far until you try it. In our day the discus, which weighs nearly four and a half pounds, has been thrown nearly one hundred and ninety-five feet. To do this, a thrower must swing his body around in circles before letting the discus fly.

This statue was first made in bronze, but the bronze has disappeared and all we have now are copies made from marble. Our picture is of one of several marble copies owned by European museums.

Myron also made a bronze cow that was so natural it is said to have fooled everyone into thinking it was a real cow. But this cow, too, has disappeared and there are not even copies left.

Bronze statues were entirely eaten away in the course of time. Marble statues often were broken, but otherwise they lasted very well.

The Discus Thrower. Museo Nazionale delle Terme, Rome.

Phidias

Ordinary men we call "Mr."—*Mr. Smith; Mr. Jones.* Great men we call by their full names without the "Mr."—George Washington, for instance. But the greatest men of all we call only by their last names. People have made lists of the hundred greatest men of all time—the greatest ruler, the greatest writer, the greatest painter, the greatest sculptor—but you may never have heard of the greatest sculptor. He was a Greek. His name was Phidias—no first name, no middle name—just Phidias.

Polyclitus and Myron made statues of men and women. Phidias made statues of gods and goddesses and godlike men and women. In Athens there is a huge, high rock called the Acropolis, which means the Upper City, and on this rock the old Greeks built a beautiful temple called the Parthenon. It was built just to hold a magnificent statue of Athene, the goddess of wisdom. The Athenians believed she watched over them and their city as a mother watches over her children, and that she gave them many useful things.

Phidias was chosen to make this statue of the goddess. Cold marble was not thought to be good enough for this statue, so Phidias made it of gold and ivory. He made it seven times as high as a human being. His *Athene* stood erect in a sleeveless robe that reached the ground. On her bosom was a breastplate with a border of serpents, because serpents were thought to be the wisest of creatures. In the center of the breastplate was the head of Medusa. (You remember that Athene helped Perseus to cut that head off.) Around the head of Medusa, between the serpents and the head, was shown a battle between the Amazons and the Greeks. Athene wore a helmet. On top of this helmet was a sphinx and on each side of the sphinx were winged horses. Athene's left arm rested on a shield and carried a lance around which coiled another serpent. In her right hand Athene held a statue of Victory, who faced her and offered her a wreath of gold. The statue of Victory was about six feet high, so you can tell how big the statue of Athene herself must have been.

This statue of Athene has entirely disappeared, probably stolen piece by piece for its gold and ivory. We know what it looked like only because we have a small, probably very poor, copy that was made of it. Judging from the copy we have, we cannot quite agree that the statue was as beautiful as the ancient Greeks thought it was.

This statue, as I told you, was on the inside of the Parthenon. All around the four outside walls of the temple, high up near the roof, was a band or strip called a frieze, or sculptured figures in low relief. This frieze was almost a tenth of a mile long and showed in marble a parade or grand procession that took place in Athens once every four years. The object of the procession was to bear a gift of a golden veil made by the virgins of Athens for their goddess. It was carried with great pomp and glory and ceremony to the temple. All Athenians—men, women, and children—took part in the procession. There were horsemen with their horses; there were animals to be sacrificed; there were girls and boys bearing gifts; there were musicians and singers.

The sculptured picture of the procession starts at one end of the Parthenon and proceeds along both sides of the temple to the other end, where the entrance is. It is the most perfect relief work that we know anything about and though there are hundreds of figures of men, women, and animals, Phidias planned it all and with his pupils made it all. Though there is a tenth of a mile of this frieze, there is not a rough or unfinished part in the whole.

When the relief was in its place on the Parthenon wall, it could barely be seen because it was so high and was closed in by the portico of columns that surrounded it. So that it might be seen better, the background and the figures were painted. But nothing except perfect work, whether it could be seen or not, was good enough for the temple of this Athenian goddess, and even the parts that never could be seen were finished perfectly.

Above and between the columns that surrounded these walls were separate groups of figures in high relief. They illustrated battles, most of them between gods and mythical, or imaginary, animals called centaurs. A centaur had the body of a horse and the head and trunk of a man. There were ninety-two groups of these spaces, or *metopes*, and there is not one of these metope sculptures that is not now broken! An arm or a leg is off, a nose is broken, an ear or an eye is missing. So you have to use your imagination to understand what the figure looked like when it was perfect.

Art Reference Bureau

At each end of the Parthenon there is a large triangular space made by the sloping roof and in these two triangular spaces were groups of superb, heroic-size figures of gods and goddesses. Heroic size means hero size—that is, bigger than real life. They are in the full round. That is, they stand free from the back. But, unfortunately again, little is left.

The group in one triangular end represented the birth of Athene. Athene supposedly was not born as a tiny baby, but full-grown and fully armed. She came from the brain of the king of the gods—that is why she was so wise. Zeus, the chief of the gods, was in the center of this group. Vulcan, the blacksmith god, had just struck him on the head with his hammer, and according to the story, Athene in full armor sprang out of his head. On each side of this central group, the other gods and goddesses are looking on. Some are standing, some are sitting, some are lying down. The groups were planned to fit the triangular spaces. Of the statues remaining, one is *Theseus*, taken from the left corner, and the so-called *Three Fates*, from the right-hand corner. *The Three Fates* are a good test of your imagination, for they have no heads, hands, or feet. Can you imagine what they once looked like?

opposite left: Phidias, Frieze from the Parthenon, **Horseman.** British Museum, London.

below: **The Three Fates.** British Museum, London.

Art Reference Bureau

Lord Elgin, an English nobleman, saw these sculptures many years ago and thought them so beautiful that he wanted his country to have them. In the position in which the frieze was placed on the Parthenon, they could not be seen properly and they were gradually being destroyed, for there seemed to be no one interested enough to take any care of them. So Lord Elgin bought most of them for what amounted to one third of a million dollars and took them to England, where they were put in the British Museum. They are known now as the Elgin marbles.

But the greatest of all the sculpture that Phidias made was not in Athens. It was in a temple at Olympia. For this temple he made a statue of Zeus. It too was made of gold and ivory, and it too has disappeared. A single lock of the statue's "hair" is said to have been worth a thousand dollars! This statue of Zeus was so famous that every Greek hoped to see it before he died. It was called one of the Seven Wonders of the World. Phidias, when he had completed it, prayed to Zeus to show in some way if he liked the statue of himself, whereupon a thunderbolt shot down from the blue sky overhead and fell at the sculptor's feet!

But the great Phidias, after all he had done, was put in prison. You'd never guess why! Because he had cut a picture of himself on the shield of *The Athene* in the Parthenon. This, to the Athenians, was a terrible crime. A mortal to put a picture of himself on the shield of their goddess! So Phidias died in prison. What an end for the greatest sculptor who ever lived!

After Phidias

Do you have a Greek nose? Do you know what a Greek nose is? It is a nose that forms a straight line from the forehead when seen from the side. Look at the people around you and see if any have Greek noses. Very few people have them today and very few of the old Greeks had them, either, but the Greek sculptors thought this kind of nose the most beautiful so they gave their statues Greek noses. A statue of the messenger of the gods, Hermes, has a perfect Greek nose.

This statue is of a strong and athletic youth. He is holding in his arms a little boy whom Zeus had given him to take care of. Hermes looks thoughtful as he tenderly holds the baby, and you can almost imagine that the baby is reaching up to pull Hermes' curly hair. He really was reaching for a bunch of grapes that Hermes held in his hand. This statue has lost parts of its arms and legs, but the head and body are still perfect and probably no broken piece of sculpture in the world is more charming or more beautiful than this. It was made by a Greek sculptor named Praxiteles (Prax-it'el-lees), and if he had made nothing else or done nothing else in his life, this one statue was great enough to make him famous through the ages.

Praxiteles is supposed to have made several other statues—one was a faun which gave the title to a book by Nathaniel Hawthorne, *The Marble Faun*—but we are not sure that there are any other sculptures in existence that he himself made.

National Tourist Organization of Greece

Praxiteles, **Hermes,
Messenger of the Gods,**
detail. Olympia Museum,
Peloponnesus, Greece.

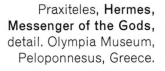

National Tourist Organization of Greece

Praxiteles, **Hermes,
Messenger of the Gods,**
detail. Olympia Museum,
Peloponnesus, Greece.

Perhaps the best-known statue in the world is one of Venus, the goddess of love and beauty, which was found on the Greek Island of Melos. It is called *The Venus of Melos* or *Venus de Milo*. She too has a perfect Greek nose, though we can't see it in the front view. We do not know who the sculptor was, but some people now think that one of the pupils of Praxiteles must have made it. This *Venus* has no arms, but a great many people have tried to imagine what the arms were doing when she did have them. Some say that she was holding a bronze shield on her knee and looking into its brightly polished surface to see herself. People had no glass mirrors at that time. Their mirrors were made of shiny metal. Others say she held a lance, or possibly nothing at all, but no one is sure.

The *Venus* was discovered not so many years ago, just by accident. A man happened to pass by a lime kiln on the island one day and the *Venus* was lying on the ground near the lime kiln. A lime kiln is a kind of furnace where stone is burned to turn it into lime. The Greek owner of the lime kiln, like many people today, saw no beauty in the old broken statue and was about to break it up and put it into the furnace to make it into lime. The man who happened by just in the nick of time *did* know how valuable the statue was and he bought it for just so much broken marble. After some time, France bought it and placed it in the Louvre in Paris. It is one of that great museum's most valuable treasures, and today could not be bought for any sum of money whatever.

Praxiteles had a friend named Scopas who also was a sculptor, but Scopas liked to make statues that showed suffering people. There are several statues of this type showing Niobe and her children which Scopas may have done. But some believe Praxiteles did them. Others think they were done by the pupils of one of these two sculptors.

Alinari-Art Reference Bureau

Alinari-Art Reference Bureau

Niobe was the mother of fourteen children—seven boys and seven girls—of whom she was very proud. But she made the mistake of boasting of them to a goddess who had only two children. That was considered a sacrilege and the goddess was jealous. As a punishment, all of Niobe's children were killed before her eyes. Niobe, with her arms about her youngest child, is shown trying to shield her from the arrows of the gods. As her last child was killed, the gods, as a great favor, turned Niobe into stone so that she wouldn't suffer any more.

One of the pupils of Scopas is supposed to have made another very famous statue which we call *The Winged Victory,* or *The Victory of Samothrace,* because it was found on the Greek island of Samothrace. The statue was made to celebrate a victory of the Greeks on the water. It shows the goddess of victory standing on the prow of a boat, the wind blowing back her robe. Though she has neither head nor arms, it is easy to imagine how she must have looked as she stood triumphantly erect, blowing a trumpet and facing the sea breeze.

You may wonder why no one has repaired this Greek statue or many of the others. As a matter of fact, many sculptors have tried to do so. Of course they were not allowed to experiment on the original statue, but they made copies and added the missing parts as they supposed those parts must have been. It may seem strange, but every such restoration, as it is called, has been so unsatisfactory that everyone prefers the broken statue instead of a restored one.

I know a little girl who always puts her hand over the illustrations in a book that she loves to read, "because," says she, "the picture I see in my mind is so much better than the picture in the book, that I don't want the picture I have in my mind spoiled!" Can you picture in your mind how the *Victory* or the *Venus* once looked?

opposite left: **Venus de Milo.** Louvre, Paris.

---

opposite right: **The Victory of Samothrace.** Louvre, Paris.

Oscar Savio, Rome

Plaster Casts

When I was a boy I used to be taken to a museum that had copies of all the great Greek sculptures, made out of plaster—called plaster casts. My favorite was a statue that was labeled *The Dying Gladiator*.

"What is a gladiator?" I asked.

A gladiator, I was told, was a swordsman, and gladiators were prisoners or slaves who were made to fight each other until one or the other died—just for the amusement of a crowd of people who gathered in a field surrounded with seats, like a football stadium, to watch the sport.

I didn't learn until later that the label on the statue was wrong, that it should have been labeled *The Dying Gaul* and

The Dying Gaul. Musei Capitolini, Rome.

Alinari-Art Reference Bureau

not *The Dying Gladiator*. The Gauls were a barbaric people who lived in the country that is now France. The Gauls fought the Greeks, and this particular Gaul was killed in battle. He wore a twisted collar around his neck called a *torque*. That's how we know he was a Gaul, for Gauls wore this particular kind of collar.

I was told that a statue called *The Apollo Belvedere* was one of the most beautiful statues of a man ever made.

Apollo, as I've told you, was the sun god and the handsomest of all the Greek gods. We don't know what he is supposed to be doing in this statue. Some say he was holding a bow in his left hand and had just pulled the bowstring with his right hand and shot a dreadful dragonlike serpent called a python that killed everyone who came near him. Others say Apollo was holding the head of Medusa in his left hand, to turn his enemy into stone. Apollo, Minerva, and Perseus all had copies of Medusa's head to kill their enemies with.

"Belvedere" means "beautiful to see," but the Apollo is called *Belvedere* because the room in which the statue now stands in the Vatican Museum in Rome is called the Belvedere Room.

I was most interested in the statues that told a story, especially if the story seemed to be something terrible. There was a big statue of three men caught in the coils of two huge serpents. It was called *The Laocoön Group*. Laocoön (Lay-ock' o-on) was a Trojan priest who told his people that the Greeks were tricking them. Just then two huge snakes attacked Laocoön's sons. He went to save them and all three were killed by the serpents. The people believed this was a sign that Laocoön was not telling the truth about their enemy, though it afterward turned out—too late—that he was right. Not *one* but *three* sculptors are said to have made this statue.

---

left: **Apollo Belvedere.** Vatican Museum, Rome.

Alinari-Art Reference Bureau

The Laocoön Group. Vatican Museum, Rome.

Oscar Savio, Rome

Boy with Thorn.
Musei Capitolini, Rome.

There was one little statue in that museum that I've always liked. It is not the statue of a god or a mythical person. It is a statue of a boy pulling a thorn out of his bare foot. Apparently boys who went barefooted two thousand years ago are very much like boys who go barefooted today!

One other statue, made just before Christ was born, was so huge that there was no plaster cast of it. It was a bronze giant statue of the sun god, about one hundred feet high, and was placed so that the god's legs straddled the entrance to a harbor in the island of Rhodes. Ships went in and out of the harbor between the legs. It was called *The Colossus of Rhodes*. It was one of the Seven Wonders of the World. For some reason, perhaps in an earthquake, *The Colossus* fell and the broken pieces were sold for junk.

Cameos, Coins, and Medals

Alinari-Art Reference Bureau

upper: Cameo from the Museo Nazionale, Naples.

middle: Cameos from the Museo Nazionale, Naples.

lower: Cameo, **Gem of Augustus.** Museo Nazionale, Rome.

I once read a description of a group of sculptured figures that had been made for a public building. The main thing the newspaper said about the sculpture was that it weighed ten tons. It did not say whether the statues were beautiful or not —just that they weighed ten tons. It might have been ten tons of coal. But mere size doesn't make a thing beautiful. The Greeks made some huge statues, but they were beautiful. They made, also, tiny sculptured figures—so small that you have to look at them under a magnifying glass to see how really beautiful they are.

Not long ago I saw in a museum a piece of such sculpture that couldn't have weighed more than an ounce and was no larger than a domino. It was a piece of colored stone through which the light shone, and was carved with beautiful figures of Greek gods and goddesses in low relief. The figures had been cut into the stone with very fine, sharp tools. It had been made before Christ was born by a Greek sculptor whose name no one knows. It was called a gem, which is the name we give to anything that is very precious, though it may be tiny.

In the British Museum in London there is a whole room of such gems made before the time of Christ by sculptors as great as those who made life-size and colossal-size figures. These gems were made for kings and wealthy people, for no one else could afford them. People who could afford it long ago used to collect such gems as you might collect postage stamps, and museums—and others who can afford it—collect them today.

Often these tiny bits of low-relief sculpture were cut in a stone that had two or three layers of different colors so that the figures were in one color and the background in another. If one layer was black and the other white, the stone was called *onyx.* If the top layer was reddish and those below it white and black, it was called *sardonyx.* Such sculptured low

Art Reference Bureau

The Portland Vase.
British Museum, London.

reliefs were known as *cameos,* and some were very beautiful. Today some cameos are made of shells of two different colors and are called shell cameos. Some are cut from two or more layers of different-colored stone cemented together or from artificial sardonyx.

It used to be the fashion for ladies to wear shell-cameo pins. Perhaps your grandmother may have had such a cameo pin. Many have profiles cut in them. Some kinds of china have white cameolike figures on a blue background. Some cameos were cut from glass of two colors. There is a famous vase in the British Museum called the Portland Vase. It is made of blue glass and the figures on it in relief are white glass. Many years ago someone knocked over the vase and it was smashed to bits. The bits were all picked up and put together again, and it was repaired so well that it is now nearly impossible to tell that it was broken.

There was another kind of gem made in great quantities before the time of Christ in which the figures were hollowed out, or sunken, instead of being raised. A gem of this sort was called a *seal*, or *intaglio*, which means sunken. The seals were used to stamp a design in wax. Of course the stamped impression made from the sunken relief was raised in wax, and one could make as many stamped impressions with the seal as he liked. Each person who could afford it had such a seal with a special design of his own to stamp everything he wished to mark with his own hand. Everyone would then know that he alone had made the impression.

The marks made by seals were used instead of signatures, back in the days when few people knew how to write—or even how to sign their names. Sometimes the seal was fitted in a finger ring that was worn by the owner so that no one else could use it. Such rings were called *signet rings*, which means "signing ring." Sometimes the seal was not mounted in a ring, but was kept in a safe place so that no one but the owner could use it.

Have you ever collected old coins—old metal money of bronze or silver? Perhaps you would never think of such coins as a kind of sculpture, but that is what old coins are—pieces of low-relief sculpture. The Greeks used to make beautiful coins with heads or figures of famous people or gods in low relief. First they made a die that was a sunken relief, and then with this die, coins were stamped out of metal—gold, silver, or bronze. One difference between a coin and a gem is that a coin is made from a die, and any number of coins all alike can be made from the same die, but there is only one of a gem. The coins of some countries today are very beautiful, but none of them are quite so beautiful as those the old Greeks made. One reason for this is that coins today have to be made quite flat, in very low relief, so that they can be stacked in a pile for the banks. It was not necessary to stack the old Greek coins in piles, so they could be made, and were made, in higher relief.

Coins were used, of course, to buy things with, but there were old coinlike sculptures called *medals* that usually were larger and were not used as money. The figures on medals were often in higher relief; they were made by pouring the metal into a mold instead of by stamping the metal with a die. Usually such medals were made for prizes in athletic games, honors in war, or to commemorate some great event, anniversary, or celebration. Medals of this kind are made today, so you may have seen one.

Alexander the Great,
from a coin.

English silver medal struck
on the victory over the
Spanish Armada, 1588.

Philip II of Macedonia,
ancient gold medallion.

Cardinal Richelieu of France,
medallion.

Seal of Philip II of Spain and
his second wife, Mary Tudor.

Historical Pictures Service, Chicago

Terra Cotta Sculpture

Alinari-Art Reference Bureau

Figurines of Tanagra.
National Museum, Athens.

Terra cotta means baked earth. A flower pot and a brick are both terra cotta—that is, earth or clay baked until it is yellowish red. The ancient Greeks made figures of people of mud or clay. They made little clay statues of women, smaller than dolls, and then baked them so that they would not crumble to pieces. That baking turned them into terra cotta.

It was then the custom to place these little figures or little statues—called figurines and statuettes—in tombs and graves. Thousands of them have been dug up and are now in museums. Since they were first dug up in a town in Greece named Tanagra, all such statuettes are called Tanagra figurines. They are usually fully clothed figures of ladies carrying a fan or a parasol.

Most of the statuettes are original, but some of them are copies of large statues. Since many of the large statues have disappeared, these figurine copies show us what the originals looked like. But they show us more than that. If you want to find out what the Greeks really were like, go to a museum and look at these little figures. The big, famous marble statues are of gods and goddesses, athletes and warriors. They were more nearly perfect than real people. But these terra cotta statuettes look like the everyday Greeks looked. One shows a girl milking a cow. Another shows two girls playing a game.

Many of the figurines were painted in bright colors. Some had tiny necklaces of real gold or held bronze ornaments in their hands. But on many of them the only color left is the yellowish red of the clay of which they are formed. The figurines are hollow except for their heads, which are solid clay.

Figurines were made for the dead, lamps were made for the living. Lamps, which every house had to have, were decorated with figures in low relief. Lamps today, of course, are usually electric and quite different from those in ancient Greece and other countries. These old lamps were very small, seldom

Alinari-Art Reference Bureau

Figurines of Tanagra. Louvre, Paris.

Alinari-Art Reference Bureau

larger than your hand, and were made either of terra cotta or bronze. There was a hole in which a twisted piece of stringlike cloth was stuffed for a wick. They held olive oil or grease which soaked the wick and made it burn when lighted. These lamps gave no more light than a burning match, but that was all the light people had at night. Perhaps they went to bed earlier than we do. The lamps often had on the top or sides the usual legendary figures—Greek gods or goddesses or other characters in Greek mythology.

Lamps were made in molds and hundreds or even thousands of lamps were made from one mold. Some of the old molds have been dug up out of the ground and are used to make modern reproductions that are sold today as souvenirs to travelers. In many cases they are sold as real antiques. If the lamps are of bronze and are really old ones that have been dug up, they have a greenish coating called a patina. If they are not really old, they are sometimes dipped in acid to make them look so, but they have sharper edges than the old and the patina made by acid does not look the same as the patina that has been eaten in by time. If they are of clay, the newly made lamps look cleaner cut and fresher than the old. So if you are thinking of buying an ancient lamp tomorrow, be sure to notice the patina or the freshness of the clay!

53

Portrait Busts and Reliefs

A bust is a piece of sculpture showing the upper part of a person—sometimes just the head and neck and sometimes the head, neck, shoulders, and chest. A bust that is made to look like a particular person is called a portrait bust.

The ancient Egyptians made some very good portrait busts, but the people who made them best were the ancient Romans. The old Roman busts are so lifelike that they look like real people you might see walking down the street today. The Greeks put Greek noses on most of their statues even though very few Greeks had Greek noses. But the Romans made their busts just like the real person. If a man had a crooked nose or a double chin, the sculptor made that man's bust with a crooked nose or double chin. If the man had a worried look, the sculptor made the bust with the worried look.

Each Roman family that could afford it had busts made of all the members of the family. These busts were handed down in the family so that an old family had a great many busts of its ancestors around the house. Whenever there was a death in the family, all the family portrait busts were carried down the street in the funeral procession. If you had watched one of those processions, you could have seen, perhaps, how much a grandson looked like the bust of his grandfather which he was carrying.

Each Roman emperor had hundreds of busts made of himself to be sent to all the important cities in the Roman Empire.

Except for the busts, the Romans weren't very good at making statues in the round. So when they conquered Greece they brought back to Rome all the famous Greek statues they could find. They brought back Greek sculptors, too, and made them carve statues in Rome. Many of the statues made in Rome were not original, but were copies of famous Greek statues. It's lucky for us that the copies were made, because so many of the great Greek statues were lost that if we hadn't been able to dig up Roman copies of them we wouldn't know at all what they were like. Do you remember Myron's *Discus Thrower*? The statue that Myron himself made disappeared and has never been found, but several Roman copies of it were made, so we know what it was like.

Alinari-Art Reference Bureau

above: Bust of **Julius Caesar.**
Museo Nazionale, Naples.

opposite: **A Roman Patrician with Busts of his Ancestors.**
Palazzo Barberini, Rome.

54

Alinari-Art Reference Bureau

The Metropolitan Museum of Art, Samuel D. Lee Fund, 1940

Alinari-Art Reference Bureau

Although the Romans weren't as good as the Greeks at making statues in the round, they did make some excellent bas reliefs. Many reliefs were made showing the campaigns of the Emperor Trajan. They show the Roman soldiers marching, camping, fighting, taking a city, capturing prisoners, and carrying off the spoils of war. Trajan's campaign was carved on a marble column and the sculptured band winds like a corkscrew round and round the column from the bottom to the top. The column is still standing in Rome. It is called Trajan's Column.

Another famous relief is carved on the Altar of the Peace of Augustus, which the Roman Senate ordered erected in 13 B.C. when the Emperor Augustus came back from putting down revolts in the western part of the Roman Empire.

Anderson-Art Reference Bureau

left: Marble bust: **Portrait head of the Emperor Caracalla.** Roman sculpture, 3rd century A.D.

above: Relief from the **Altar of Peace.** Uffizi, Florence.

right: Column of Trajan, Rome.

Stories in Stone

What would you call men who went about with hammers and broke all the statues they could find, and who even went into churches and broke the statues there?

Long ago (about 800 A.D.) such men broke statues because they thought statues were too much like idols. They thought a church especially should have nothing like an idol or an image in it. An image is called in Greek an *icon* and these men were called *iconoclasts*, which means "image smashers." They smashed a great many statues, and the sculptors were forced to move away from the cities where the iconoclasts were if they still wanted to make statues.

The iconoclasts, however, didn't seem to mind small sculptures in relief. And so during this time, and for many years afterward, many beautiful bas reliefs in ivory, silver, and gold were made. The carvings in ivory were used as the covers of books, writing tablets, and little boxes. Many of them are now in museums where they are kept carefully in glass cases. When you look at them, remember the iconoclasts and why there were no good statues in the full round for a long time after the Romans.

Some sculptors had to leave Byzantium—the old name for Constantinople which was the old name for Istanbul—because of the iconoclasts. They traveled to France and carried on their work there.

And it is to France that we turn for our next great statues. They belong to the Middle Ages, several hundred years after the iconoclasts. And, strangely enough, these statues were all carved for churches—just what the iconoclasts didn't want! In fact, the churches were covered with statues, which were made of the same kind of stone as the buildings and not of marble like the Greek and Roman statues. These statues were really part of the churches. The cathedral at Chartres, in France, has at least ten thousand figures of men and animals on it. They are everywhere—over the doorways, on the columns, on the roof, under the windows, on the walls. Even the waterspouts are carved in the forms of strange animals.

Most of the people of the Middle Ages could neither read nor write; all these sculptures on the churches took the place of books. They told the people stories of the Bible and of the saints. They were useful as well as ornamental.

Gothic figures from the Cathedral at Chartres.

French Government Tourist Office, Chicago

They are called Gothic figures because churches and cathedrals of the Middle Ages were built in the Gothic style. The Gothic figures on the cathedral are of almost every kind of living thing you could think of. There are scenes from the Bible, statues of saints, carvings of animals and flowers, pictures in stone of the seasons, of different kinds of work like farming and writing, wood chopping and fighting. There are figures of men and women, of actual creatures and of strange unheard-of make-believe creatures. And each of these figures was made for that particular part of the cathedral where it was placed. They were a part of it, built into it, and made of the same stone.

On the Gothic churches there are statues that "gargle" every time it rains. They are rain spouts with holes in them so water can run out through their mouths. Like the statues that told the stories of the Bible, they are useful as well as ornamental. We call them *gargoyles*, which is another way of saying they gargle.

The gargoyles were carved in the shapes of very strange animals. Some have heads like monkeys, some have three heads, some have their tongues sticking out as if they were making faces. Some have claws like eagles, others hands like men.

The strange animals that weren't made to gargle are called *grotesques*. Most of them are up near the roof like the gargoyles and seem to be looking down and laughing at the people on the ground.

Gargoyles from the Cathedral of Notre Dame, Paris.

French Government Tourist Office, Chicago

The Gates of Paradise

This story begins with a competition. Not a competition to see who could run the fastest, not a competition to see who could whistle loudest, but a much more difficult one. It was such a difficult competition that each man who entered was given a year in which to try to win.

It was a competition in sculptures. It began this way: In Florence, Italy, there is a little eight-sided building called the Baptistery. A baptistery is a place where babies are baptized. This building has four doorways. One of these doorways at the time of the competition had a very beautiful pair of bronze doors with reliefs made by the sculptor Andrea Pisano. Long after Andrea Pisano's death the men of Florence decided there should be another pair of bronze doors for one of the other doorways.

There were several good sculptors living then and the men of Florence could not decide who was the best one to make the new doors. So they had the competition. These were the rules:

Each sculptor had to make a relief in bronze to go on a door.

The relief had to be about Abraham and Isaac.

Each sculptor could have a year for the work, and then a group of thirty-four judges would decide the winner and the winner would make the doors.

All the sculptors set to work. All, except one, very carefully kept everyone else from seeing their work until the year was up. This one was named Lorenzo Ghiberti (Gee-bear'tee). He worked and worked, and then asked his friends to come in and tell him how he could make his relief better. Then he worked some more until he had a very beautiful relief indeed.

When the year was up each sculptor brought his relief to the judges. And what do you think? The judges couldn't decide which was the very best! There was a tie for first place. One of the winners was Ghiberti's relief. The other was cast by the famous architect Brunelleschi (Brew-nel-less'kee). But Brunelleschi himself thought Ghiberti's relief was better than his own and so he very generously said he would withdraw and let Ghiberti be the winner. Then the judges said Ghiberti could make the doors.

Alinari-Art Reference Bureau

Ghiberti, bronze doors, detail. Baptistery, Florence.

Alinari-Art Reference Bureau

right: Ghiberti, bronze doors. Baptistery, Florence.

Ghiberti set to work. He worked and worked. One year, two years, five years, *ten years*, and still he worked on the doors. He started to work on the reliefs in 1403. He finished the doors in 1424.

Twenty-one years to make one pair of doors? That *is* a long time!

Finally the doors were finished and put in the Baptistery. They opened down the middle and had twenty-eight panels, or scenes, in relief, most of them from the life of Christ. Each scene was made separately and then they were all fitted together.

Everyone liked Ghiberti's doors so much that the men of Florence asked the sculptor to make another pair of bronze doors for another doorway to the Baptistery. There was no need for a competition this time. They knew Ghiberti was the man for the job.

Ghiberti started on the new doors. He worked and worked. One year, two years, five years, ten years, *twenty years*, and still he worked on the doors. He began on these doors in 1425. He finished them in 1452. Twenty-seven years to make the second set of doors!

But this time, when he had finished, the doors were so splendid that many people said they were perfect. A famous sculptor saw them and said, "They are fit to be the gates of Paradise," and that is what they have been called ever since— *The Gates Of Paradise. The Gates of Paradise* have ten scenes from the Old Testament.

Some Renaissance Sculptors

After the Middle Ages, the whole world got spring fever, the full-of-energy kind of spring fever, and it lasted not for just a few days in spring but for many years.

Italy caught the fever first, in about 1400. Just as life is born again in the spring after the dark winter and blossoms forth in green leaves and bright flowers, so new life was born again in painting, architecture, writing, sculpture, exploration, discovery, trade, and everything else, and blossomed forth after the dark of the Middle Ages.

This "Born Again" time we call the *Renaissance*—a word that means rebirth.

One of the germs that had made the world catch this Renaissance fever was the interest people began to take in the skill and learning of ancient times. Statues and buildings that had been buried in the ground since Roman times were dug up. Old Roman and Greek writings were brought to light and read again. When it was learned what the Ancients had done in art the Renaissance people themselves did some great things in art.

One of the first sculptors to make a thorough study of the Roman statues was named Donatello. He lived in Florence, but when still a very young man, he went to Rome with his friend Brunelleschi. In Rome the two friends spent their time hunting through the old ruins for any beautiful Roman work they could find. Brunelleschi was interested in architecture; he measured the old Roman buildings while Donatello looked for sculpture. Soon people called them "the treasure hunters" because they always seemed to be looking for buried treasure.

When the two treasure hunters came back to Florence, Donatello made a beautiful marble gallery for singers, for the wall at one end of the cathedral. The outside of the gallery he filled with sculpture of little children, who look like cupids, dancing and singing. It is a very wonderful piece of work, full of life and action.

Donatello's next famous statue was set up on the outside of a church in Florence. It is of Saint George. Saint George was a Christian in the Roman army at a time when it was very dangerous to be a Christian. To show that he was not afraid of

Alinari-Ente Provinciale per il Turismo, Florence

being called a Christian, he wore on his shield a bright red cross with a white background. Ever since, this has been called the Cross of Saint George. It is a part of the flag of England, for Saint George was adopted by the English as their favorite saint. He was a brave man and when the Roman emperor began to persecute the Christians, Saint George went to him and asked him to stop. For this, and because Saint George was a Christian, the emperor had him killed.

Of course Donatello didn't know what the real Saint George looked like, as he had lived so long before, so this statue is not a portrait statue. It is what Donatello thought a fine, brave young Christian officer in the Roman army ought to look like. So many other people thought this was what Saint George ought to look like that the statue became very famous. It is very lifelike.

"There is only one trouble with it," someone told Donatello.

"What is that?" asked the sculptor, who was afraid the man had found some fault in the statue.

"The trouble is it can't speak," said the man.

Donatello's most famous work was of a man on horseback. I'll tell you about that in the next chapter.

A sculptor who was a friend of Donatello's had a secret. He didn't tell anyone except his adopted son. The adopted son had five sons of his own and when they grew up they were let into the secret, too. It was a family secret.

The sculptor who had the secret in the first place was named Luca della Robbia. Like Donatello, he lived in Florence. He was a little younger than Donatello and so we call him the second great sculptor of the Renaissance. Luca della Robbia made statues in marble and bronze. One of his works in marble was a gallery to go on the end wall in the cathedral, opposite Donatello's marble gallery.

Donatello, **St. George.**

Alinari-Ente Provinciale per il Turismo, Florence

Luca della Robbia, **The Singing Gallery,** details. Museo di S. Maria del Fiore, Florence.

Alinari-Ente Provinciale per il Turismo, Florence

Luca della Robbia, **The Singing Gallery.** Museo di S. Maria del Fiore, Florence.

Luca della Robbia carved singing boys on this gallery just as Donatello had on the other one. The two galleries are called *The Singing Galleries*. Luca della Robbia's looks better than Donatello's when you are close to it because Donatello's is rougher—not so smoothly finished. But when you are as far away from the galleries as you would be on the floor of the cathedral, Donatello's figures stand out better because they are rougher. So it's about even between them.

They are both so valuable that they are now in a museum instead of in the cathedral.

But we've almost forgotten about the secret. Luca della Robbia found that it took a great deal of time to carve in marble, and marble was very expensive to buy. When he got through and was paid for his work, he usually found he hadn't made much money. Bronze had the same drawbacks. He decided to try to find some material that could be used quickly and that was inexpensive. He found it. What do think it was? Not wood or stone, and of course not marble or bronze, but clay.

Luca della Robbia used terra cotta, but here his secret comes in. After he finished the clay statue, he put over it a coating of porcelain, which is something like glass. Then he baked the figures in an oven for just the right length of time. His secret was in mixing the porcelain, or *glaze*, as it was called. When it was finished it would last in the rain and bad weather just as well as marble, whereas the terra cotta without the glaze would soon crumble away. Other sculptors tried it, but none did such fine work in glazed terra cotta as Luca della Robbia. His secret glazing process was very successful.

Most of the sculpture Luca della Robbia did in glazed terra cotta was in relief. The relief part was usually white, like marble, but the background was a beautiful shade of blue.

Luca della Robbia taught his nephew, whom he had adopted as a son, the secret of the glazed terra cotta. The nephew's name was Andrea della Robbia. Andrea became almost as famous as Luca. Andrea did most of his work in glazed terra cotta and he added many more colors to his reliefs, although he usually left the flesh part of his statues white. His best examples were reliefs of the Madonna and Child.

For the outside of a children's hospital in Florence, Andrea did a series of terra cotta high reliefs of babies in swaddling clothes. Each baby is on a separate round background. You may have seen plaster casts of these babies, but the plaster casts are white, and do not show the colors that Andrea della Robbia put on the originals. Each baby is called a *bambino*, the Italian word for baby.

Andrea della Robbia, **Bambino,** Florence.

Alinari-Ente Provinciale per il Turismo, Florence

Italian State Tourist Office-Enit. Foto Enit-Roma.

Two Equestrian Statues

In the days when men used horses to carry them from place to place, many statues were made showing great men on horseback.

The reason there are no statues of men in automobiles is that a large man-made article like an automobile is not a suitable subject for sculpture. Very few man-made articles are. A sculptor tries to copy nature. His subjects are things that grow —men, animals, plants, flowers. A good mechanic with a hammer and chisel could carve an automobile in marble, but it takes an artist to model a horse.

You remember the horses and their riders made by Phidias on the Parthenon frieze? They are reliefs. It is much easier to make a horse in relief than in the round, because in the relief the horse is part of the background and does not have to support all its weight on its legs. A statue of a man on horseback is called an *equestrian* statue. The Romans made better equestrian statues than the Greeks because they knew more about supporting weights. But after the time of the ancient Romans no good equestrian statue was made for a thousand years.

The man who made the first good equestrian statue after all those years was Donatello. It was bigger than life-size and was made of bronze. It took Donatello ten years to make it and set it up in Padua, Italy. It is such a fine statue that many people call it the second best equestrian statue in the world. The man on the horse was Gattamelata, so Donatello's statue is called *The Gattamelata*.

Notice how heavy and strong the horse is. Gattamelata was a soldier and soldiers' horses in the time of the Renaissance were true war horses—strong enough to carry the weight of a man in armor, and heavy enough to charge with great force like the heavy halfbacks on a football team. I have never seen a real horse with his foot on a ball, and Donatello hadn't either, but he had to put the ball there to make the heavy statue steady. See what a well-balanced easy seat in the saddle the rider has.

Donatello, **The Gattamelata**, Padua.

Ente Provinciale per il Turismo, Venice

If the Gattamelata is the second best equestrian statue in the world, what is the best one? Think of all the sculptors who might have made the finest man on horseback. Think of all the hundreds or even thousands of years since sculpture began, and you will be astonished to learn that the best and the next best equestrian statues were both made during the Renaissance; they were both made by goldsmiths; they were both made by men who lived in Florence; they were both statues of soldiers on war horses, and they were both set up in cities in Italy not very far from Florence.

The best statue was made by a sculptor known as Verrocchio (Ver-rok'-kee-o). Verrocchio was not his real name. It was the name of the man who taught him to be a goldsmith. Strangely enough, Verrocchio in Italian means "true eye." Certainly he lived up to his name. The statue is of a soldier who was commander-in-chief of the armies of Venice. His name was Colleoni (Kol-lay-o'nee). Donatello's *Gattamelata*, Verrocchio's *Colleoni*.

Colleoni was a fine general. He commanded his soldiers well and fought well. He was very strong. He could race with his armor on against the fastest runners in the whole army. He liked to study, he encouraged artists and students at his camp, he was very courteous. He never ate too much or slept too much, and he was noted for his strict honesty.

When Colleoni died, it was found that he had left all his fortune to the Republic of Venice on condition that Venice set up a statue of him in the square of St. Mark. To put a statue there was against the law of Venice, so the Venetians thought they wouldn't get his fortune after all. Then they had a bright idea. They remembered a building called the School of St. Mark which had a little square in front of it.

"Why can't that be called the Square of St. Mark too?" they said. So they had Verrocchio make the statue and put it there, and in this way they got the money left by Colleoni.

Verrocchio balanced the statue so well that no ball had to be put under the uplifted forefoot of his horse. Because the statue was on a high pedestal, the sculptor exaggerated Colleoni's features so they would look right when seen from the ground.

Verrocchio's *Colleoni* is one of the most glorious pieces of sculpture in the world, and the best equestrian statue.

Verrocchio, **Colleoni,** Venice.

Brogi-Art Reference Bureau

Michelangelo Buonarroti

Today there is no famous sculptor who is also a famous painter. But in 1475 a man was born who became world famous as a sculptor, as a painter, and as an architect. He was also a poet and wrote verses that are still published. Not only that, but he is considered the greatest artist of the Renaissance. Many people call him the greatest sculptor since Phidias.

The name of this wonderful genius was Buonarroti (Boo-own-ar-rot'ee). Have you ever heard before of Buonarroti? Very few people know him by that name. He is better known to us as Michelangelo. Michelangelo was trained as a sculptor in marble and he always spoke of himself as a sculptor in spite of the fact that his most famous works are the paintings in the Sistine Chapel in Rome. As a boy he carved a statue in snow that greatly pleased one of the famous Medici family, the Duke of Florence. The boy was permitted to study the old Greek and Roman statues collected by the duke, who later gave him work to do.

When Michelangelo was still a young man, he carved in marble a wonderful statue called *The Pietà*. This piece of work shows Mary, the mother of Jesus, holding her dead son across her lap after his crucifixion. Some people like it better than Michelangelo's other works because it is calmer, more quiet and tranquil, than statues he did afterward.

Some time after making *The Pietà*, Michelangelo was able to do a piece of work that made him famous throughout Italy. There lay in Florence a huge block of marble that an earlier sculptor had begun to work on, but had been unable to finish because the marble was so long and narrow.

Michelangelo offered to make a statue out of this block of marble. He was given permission to carve it, and he went to work. The block was set up on end and enclosed with a fence so that Michelangelo could work in peace. In three years he had finished. People came in crowds to see what he had done.

It was a colossal statue eighteen feet high, showing David with his sling ready to fight Goliath the giant. Strange to say, every-

Michelangelo, **David.** Accademia, Florence.

Alinari·Art Reference Bureau

one in Florence called the statue "The Giant," although it was of a man who killed a giant. It is gigantic in size. It weighs nine tons.

Michelangelo was a very careful student of anatomy, the study of the muscles and other parts of the body. He studied the bodies of people and even cut up dead bodies so he could learn about the muscles under the skin that would make a statue look lifelike. He knew so much about muscles that he carved some of his statues in strained and unusual positions, showing the proper play of muscles under the skin.

For the tomb of one of the popes, Michelangelo carved a statue of Moses. Of course he did not know what Moses really looked like. He had no pictures of Moses to go by, so the Moses he carved is the sculptor's idea of what a man like Moses ought to look like. Michelangelo carved horns on his Moses! You can see them in the picture. The Bible says the face of Moses shone with light when he came down from Mount Sinai. In early Italian translations of the Bible, the rays of light coming from the head of Moses were called by the translators "horns." And for this reason people of Michelangelo's time thought Moses had horns. The statue is forceful, majestic, powerful. All who see it remember it. Travelers have said it is as impressive as seeing Niagara Falls or the ocean or a storm at sea.

As famous as Michelangelo's *Moses* are the groups of statues that he made for the tombs of two members of the Medici family. These tombs are in the Medicis' private chapel, in the church of San Lorenzo. Michelangelo placed two figures, a man and a woman, on each tomb. Above these, in a niche in the wall, was placed a statue of the man whose tomb it was. One of these portrait statues is known as *The Thinker* and the other as *The Warrior*. The two figures on one of the tombs are known as *Morning* and *Evening* and those on the other as *Day* and *Night*.

Michelangelo lived to be eighty-nine; he died in 1564.

Strange to say, sculpture got worse instead of better after Michelangelo, and it was many years before it began to improve.

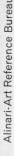

left: Michelangelo, **Moses**. S. Pietro Vincoli, Rome.

---

right column, top to bottom:

Michelangelo, **Morning,** Medici Chapel, Florence.

Michelangelo, **Evening,** Medici Chapel, Florence.

Michelangelo, **Night,** Medici Chapel, Florence.

Michelangelo, **Day,** Medici Chapel, Florence.

Alinari-Art Reference Bureau

Cellini Makes his Perseus

A man named Benvenuto Cellini (Chel-lee'nee) became known as the best goldsmith in Italy. His work in gold and silver and precious stones was so wonderful that the few examples we have now are all in museums and are considered priceless.

Cellini was a goldsmith, but he believed he could do good sculpture too, and although he was very boastful about it, he made good every boast, for his bronze statues turned out to be just as good as he said they would be.

Cellini lived in Florence and the Duke of Florence asked him to make a bronze statue of Perseus killing Medusa. Cellini worked hard and long on the clay model for the Perseus until he thought it was just right. Then came the work of casting the statue in bronze.

Today when a sculptor wants to make a bronze statue, he makes a clay model first and then sends it to the bronze foundry, where the statue is cast in bronze. This is easier for the sculptor because he can spend all his time modeling statues and not have to do also the work of bronze casting. But during the Renaissance a sculptor like Cellini usually had to make the bronze cast himself, as well as the clay model. This was often a very hard thing for a sculptor to do.

Cellini's statue of Perseus and Medusa was to be larger than life-size and many people in Florence said that it would be impossible for Cellini, a goldsmith, to make a good bronze casting of such a big statue. Even the Duke of Florence told Cellini he thought it would be unwise for a goldsmith, who is used to working with tiny jewels, to cast a large bronze statue.

All this discussion, however, made Cellini very anxious to do the bronze statue. He began by building a furnace in which to melt the bronze. Then he dug a pit in which to put the mold and connected it with tubes so the melted bronze could run down into the mold and harden. The mold was just the shape of the statue. To make it easier, Cellini cast the Medusa part of the statue first. The Medusa turned out very well indeed.

Then Cellini began the casting of Perseus. This was much harder to do, because of its greater size and peculiar shape. The fire in the furnace melting the bronze got so hot that the roof of Cellini's house caught fire. Cellini himself had to work like fury to keep the fire burning in the furnace. He became so exhausted and ill that he had to go to bed. From there he supervised his helpers and told them just what to do. He felt so sick he thought he was going to die.

Before long, one of the helpers came to Cellini's room and told him that the statue was ruined, for the bronze was not melting right. Cellini, in spite of his sickness, jumped out of bed and dashed to the furnace. He was a very hot-tempered man and now he was in such a rage with his stupid helpers that he frightened them so they jumped every time he spoke.

A storm had come up and it began to rain. Cellini sent two men out for more wood for the furnace fire and then the fire got so hot that the roof caught again. Cellini ordered some of the helpers to put up boards or carpets to help keep off the rain. Then they stirred the bronze with long iron rods until it began to be the right thickness again.

Suddenly there was a great flash of light and the crash of an explosion. They were all too frightened to move. Then Cellini saw that the cap of the furnace had blown off and the bronze was bubbling over the top. So he quickly opened the tubes that would let the metal flow into the mold below.

Still the bronze didn't flow freely. Cellini thought the great heat had eaten up the metal that was mixed with the copper to make it flow. What was he to do?

He gathered together all the pewter platters, bowls, and dishes in the house and threw them into the melting bronze. Pewter is a soft metal that was often used for dishes. The pewter melted and mixed with the bronze. The bronze flowed and soon the mold was filled. The scheme had worked. Cellini was so pleased that he forgot all about his sickness and felt as well as ever.

Here is the picture of the finished statue of Perseus killing Medusa, cast in bronze with so much bragging and trouble and excitement, by Cellini. Perseus holds up the head which he has just cut off. He is not looking at it, because that would turn him to stone. Notice the strange-looking sword. Notice that Cellini has made the blood flowing from Medusa in bronze, too.

The statue was set up in Florence and there it still stands, admired all the more by those who know how hard Cellini worked to cast it.

upper right: Cellini, **Perseus and Medusa.** Loggia dei Lanzi, Florence.

lower right: Cellini, **Gold Rospigliosi Cup.**

Italian State Tourist Office-Enit. Foto Ente Provinciale per il Turismo, Florence.

Metropolitan Museum of Art, Bequest of Benjamin Altman, 1913.

right: Goujon, **Water Nymph panels from the Fountain of the Innocents,** Paris.

far right: Giovanni Bologna, **Mercury.**

Historical Pictures Service, Chicago

After Michelangelo

What goes up must come down. Sculpture had been going up. It had been getting better and better and better since the beginning of the Renaissance. Renaissance sculpture went way up to the top under the great Michelangelo. Then it came down!

For two hundred years after Michelangelo there were hundreds of sculptors, but only a very few good ones. One of these good ones was Cellini, the goldsmith who made the bronze Perseus.

There were two more good sculptors after Michelangelo who were not Italians like almost all the other great Renaissance sculptors. One, named Jean Goujon (Goo-jonh'), was born in France. The other, called John of Bologna (Bo-lon'ya), came from the town of Douai in Flanders.

Goujon is best known for some beautiful water nymphs that he carved in very low relief. Each nymph is carved on a separate strip or panel of marble; they were used to decorate the Fountain of the Innocents in Paris.

I told you that John of Bologna was born in Flanders, but he didn't stay there. He moved to Italy and lived in Italy the rest of his life. All his important work was done in Italy. Because a famous fountain he made was placed in the city of Bologna in Italy, people began to think he was a man of Bologna and called him Giovanni da Bologna, which means John of Bologna.

Giovanni da Bologna made a statue called *The Flying Mercury* that is his masterpiece. Mercury looks as if he were running in the air as well as flying with his winged cap and sandals and *caduceus*. The caduceus is Mercury's staff or wand that has two snakes curling round it. Mercury was believed to be the messenger of the gods. He was also the god of commerce and hospitality and flocks and herds and speech-making and sly tricks and dreams and peace and traveling and health and riches. The Greeks believed he invented the alphabet and numbers and astronomy and music and boxing and weights and measures and gymnastics and growing olive orchards. So you see what an important fellow he was. His caduceus is often used as the sign of doctors because Mercury was the god of health. When animals or people quarreled the caduceus was supposed to make them friends again. Mercury once saw two snakes fighting. He threw his staff down between them and the two snakes curled peacefully around it. So Mercury kept them there to show the power of his staff.

National Gallery of Art, Washington, D.C., Andrew Mellon Collection, 1937.

Canova and Thorvaldsen

Alinari-Art Reference Bureau

Swiss National Tourist Office

Antonio Canova was the best Italian sculptor after the time of Michelangelo. We usually call him simply Canova. He lived from 1757 to 1822.

Canova was brought up by his grandparents and because his grandfather was a stone cutter, the boy from the beginning had a chance to be a sculptor. When he was only eight years old he carved in marble two small shrines. When he was about ten, he is said to have carved a lion out of butter for the banquet of a rich nobleman, who liked it so much that he became Canova's patron, or backer.

Canova studied hard to become a sculptor and by the time he was a man he was doing a great many good statues. These brought him much fame and much money. The money he spent by giving it away to poor people, founding art schools, helping sculptors, and giving prizes for good sculpture.

Canova's statues are very smooth and pretty, but not very strong in appearance. He carved a great many statues of the ancient gods and goddesses and seemed to imitate the old Greek and Roman art. He also carved portrait busts of famous men, including George Washington.

Canova's *Perseus* with the head of Medusa looks a little like another *Perseus*. Canova's *Perseus* isn't as good as Cellini's, but probably it is just as famous.

In 1797, when Canova was at the height of his fame, there came to Italy a young man from Denmark. He liked Italy so much he stayed there for twenty-three years and soon became famous as a sculptor. Perhaps you have seen pictures of the dying lion he carved in solid rock—the famous *Lion of Lucerne*. It was made by a *Danish* sculptor in *Italy* in honor of the *Swiss* guards who died in *France* rather than surrender. That certainly is a mixture of countries!

left: Canova, **Perseus and Medusa.** Vatican, Rome.

right: Thorvaldsen, **The Lion of Lucerne,** Lucerne.

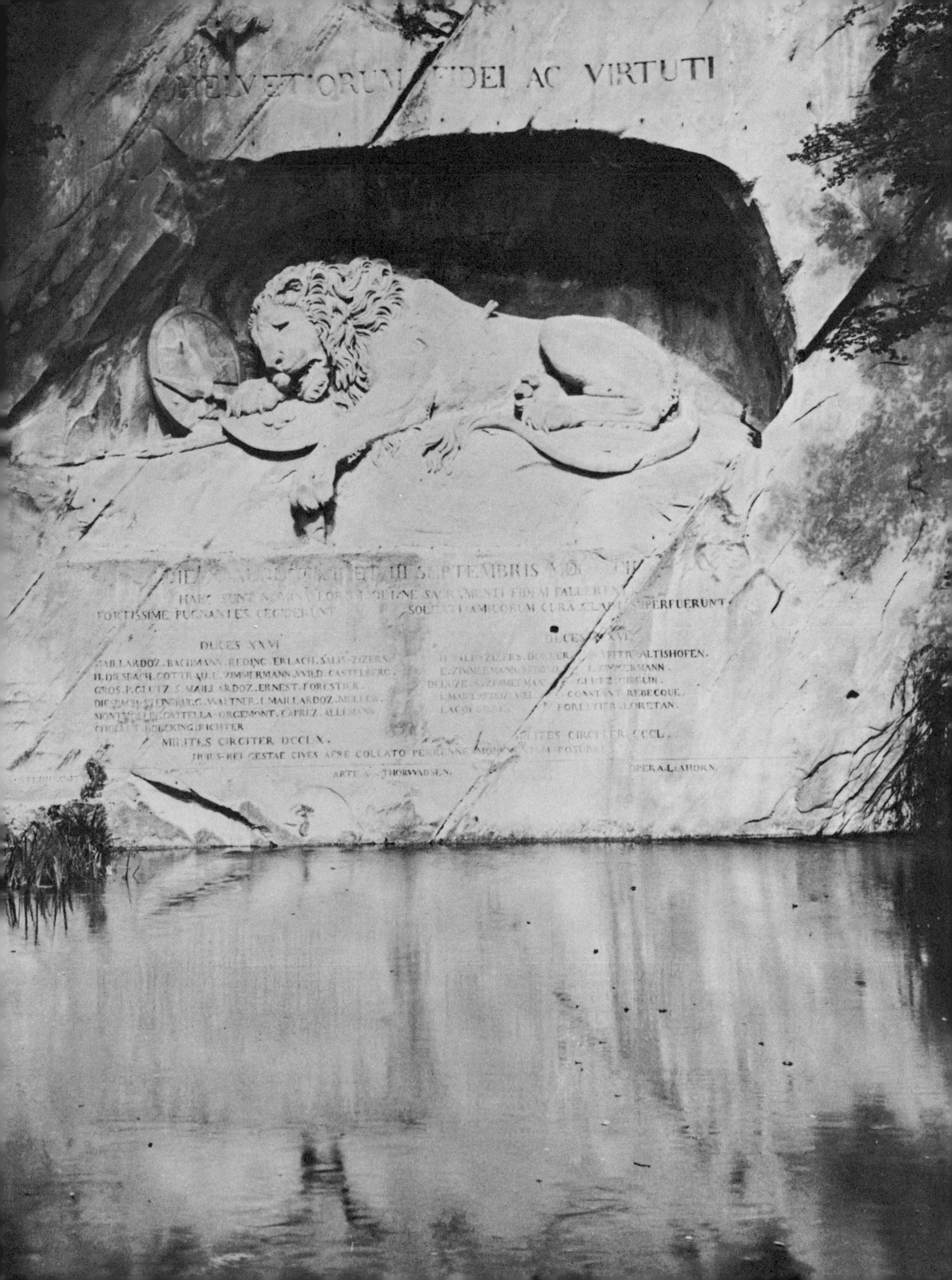
AC VIRTUTI
DUCES XXVI
MILITES CIRCITER DCCLX
ARTE

Thorvaldsen, **Christ,** Baltimore, Maryland.

The Johns Hopkins Medical Institutions

The Dane's name was Thorvaldsen (Tor'valt-sen). He knew Canova and, like Canova, imitated the style of the statues of ancient Greece and Rome. He was the most successful of the imitators. Some of his works, however, like *The Lion of Lucerne,* were not in ancient style.

When Thorvaldsen returned from a visit to Denmark after twenty-three years abroad, he had become so famous that he was asked to make a colossal statue of Christ and twelve colossal statues of the Apostles for a church in Copenhagen. Colossal, you remember, means tremendously large, like *The Colossus of Rhodes*. These huge statues were completed in Italy in twenty years and sent to Copenhagen. A copy of the Christ stands in the lobby of the Johns Hopkins Hospital in Baltimore.

When Thorvaldsen died, he left much of his fortune for the building of an art museum in Copenhagen. There most of his works are kept, and the sculptor himself is buried in the courtyard.

Portrait Statues by Houdon

If you collect stamps I'm sure you have at least one with a side view, or profile, of George Washington's head. This side view of Washington's head was first used on postage stamps in 1851. It has been used on many issues of ordinary United States postage stamps since then. Sometimes it has been a three-cent stamp, sometimes a two-cent, and sometimes a one-cent stamp that has had this Washington head on it.

All these profile pictures on stamps were made from a bust of Washington. The bust was made from Washington himself at Mount Vernon. It was made by a sculptor who was an expert at making busts that looked like the real people.

This expert was a Frenchman named Jean Antoine Houdon (Oo-donh). Houdon was one of the best sculptors France had had for two hundred years. When he was a boy he studied art in Paris and when he was twenty he won a prize for sculpture. The prize gave him enough money to study art in Italy for four years. He liked Italy and stayed there ten years instead of four. Then he came back to France.

Houdon said he believed a sculptor should try to make true likenesses of men who had brought glory and honor to their country so that people would always know what these men looked like. Houdon became just as successful at making portrait statues as the Romans had been. Some people think he was even better than the Romans. The most famous statue Houdon made was of a French writer named Voltaire. Voltaire is shown seated in a chair.

Have you ever wondered why so many statues have eyes without pupils? One reason the eyes are blank is that the sculptor tried to make the exact shape of the eyes. As you know, there isn't any hole in the outside material of a real eyeball, and the sculptor felt it would not be right to make a hole in the statue's eyeball. If a sculptor wanted to show the iris (the colored part) and the pupil (the black center) he painted them on the eyes or put glass or crystal eyeballs in the statue. Carving the eyes without pupils was good sculpture, but it did make the eyes look blank. Michelangelo very lightly carved a circle and dot on his David's eyes, but most of his other statues have blank eyes.

Historical Pictures Service, Chicago

Houdon, bust of **George Washington,** Mt. Vernon, Fairfax County, Virginia.

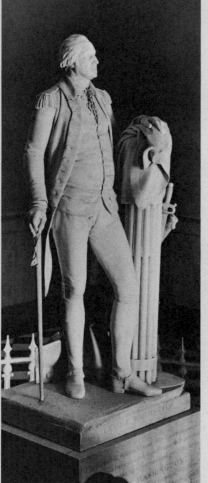

Virginia Department of Conservation and Economic Development

Now, Houdon thought that a portrait statue ought to have eyes with iris and pupil. So Houdon invented a way of doing this. He made a deep hole for the pupil and made the iris in relief. He also left some of the marble for the white part of the eye a little raised so that it would catch the light. Houdon's scheme worked very well. His portrait busts look very much alive. Some of the busts even seem to have a twinkle in their eyes.

When Benjamin Franklin was in France he had his portrait bust made by Houdon. Franklin liked the bust of himself so much that he asked Houdon to come to the new United States to make a statue of George Washington. It took Houdon and Franklin almost two months to sail from France to America. That was a fast trip in 1785! Some of the side views of Franklin on United States postage stamps have been taken from Houdon's bust of Franklin.

Houdon went to Mount Vernon and stayed with Washington until he had made the bust that the postage stamps are copied from. This bust has never left Mount Vernon and it can still be seen at the home of Washington. Then Houdon made a full-length marble statue of Washington which is now in the Capitol at Richmond, Virginia.

Besides busts of Voltaire, Franklin, and Washington, Houdon made busts of John Paul Jones, Thomas Jefferson, Lafayette, and many other people—men, women, and children.

And now, even if you are not a stamp collector, you know more about the portrait on one stamp than many stamp collectors know.

Houdon, **George Washington,** Richmond, Virginia.

Barye, Frémiet, and Vela

Do you like to go to the zoo? Almost everyone likes to look at animals or hunt animals or play with animals or draw animals. A man named Barye (Ba-ree) liked to make statues of animals.

Barye lived in Paris. He worked in a jewelry shop and was a goldsmith, as were so many of the Renaissance sculptors of Florence. But Barye lived in the 1800's, much later than the Renaissance.

Barye loved to go to the zoo in Paris. He used to take paper and crayons to the zoo and draw pictures of the animals. Then he would go home and make little statues of the animals he had drawn. When he was at work in the jewelry shop, he often made tiny gold animals for watch chains and necklaces and bronze animals to go on clocks. In this way Barye practised until he became the best animal sculptor of his time in the world. His lions and tigers were especially liked by Americans and on the street corners of American towns men used to sell plaster casts of Barye's *Walking Lion.*

Many of Barye's bronzes show pain and cruelty. He seemed to like to make statues such as a tiger eating an alligator or a jaguar eating a rabbit.

Many of Barye's bronze animals are much too small for monuments, but people call his work monumental sculpture. This means that Barye modeled his statues in the same way large monuments should be modeled. They are not filled with tiny details and are heavy in shape. "Heavy in shape" doesn't mean they are not graceful, but it does mean that a Barye bronze looks beautiful even at a distance as well as near at hand—monumental.

Almost as good as Barye at making animal statues was still another Frenchman. His name was Frémiet (Fray-mee-ay). Frémiet made many splendid statues of animals. In one called *Pan and the Two Bear Cubs,* Pan is tickling the little bears with a straw.

Frémiet made statues of people as well as animals. His statues of men on horseback—equestrian statues—proved to be his best ones. His most famous equestrian statue is his *Joan of Arc.* Joan is clad in armor and holds aloft the flag of the King of France as she leads the king's soldiers to battle.

The Metropolitan Museum of Art, Rogers Fund, 1910.

above: Barye, **Walking Lion.**

opposite: Frémiet, **Joan of Arc,** Paris.

below: Frémiet, **Pan and the Two Bear Cubs.** Musee National du Luxembourg, Paris.

Frenchmen are proud of Joan of Arc. They consider her a saint. Frenchmen are proud, too, of another leader of French armies, although he certainly wasn't a saint. His name was Napoleon.

You probably already know the story of Napoleon, the boy from Corsica who went to a military school, became a lieutenant in the French army, then a famous and successful general. He made himself Emperor of France and became the most powerful man of his time in all the world. At last he was defeated and went to live on Elba, an island in the Mediterranean. From Elba he suddenly returned to France. His old soldiers rallied round him. He raised an army to fight the English and the Prussians. He was beaten at the battle of Waterloo and sent to the island of St. Helena, far away in the South Atlantic Ocean. There Napoleon spent the last six years of his life, longing to return to lead his armies once more to victory. And there he died.

Historical Pictures Service, Chicago

French Government Tourist Office, Chicago

Historical Pictures Service, Chicago

Vela, **The Last Days of Napoleon I.** Chateau, Versailles.

This statue shows Napoleon at St. Helena, a map of Europe spread on his knees, one hand clenched in rage at his loss of power, the other hand loosely open, showing how hopeless he feels his chance of returning is.

The statue was done by a sculptor named Vincenzio Vela, who was born in Switzerland. It is called a dramatic statue because it shows something happening. It is not just Napoleon, but Napoleon wishing to return and win back his past glory.

The Statue of Liberty

Have you ever been inside a statue? Most big bronze statues are hollow and often there is room inside for a man—if there were any way of getting in. But there is only one statue in the world that hundreds of thousands of people have been inside of. Forty people *can* get into the head at one time. The one I'm talking about, of course, is *The Statue of Liberty*.

The Statue of Liberty stands on a stone base or pedestal. The pedestal stands on a little island at the entrance of New York Harbor. Every ship that goes in or out of New York passes near the statue. Even in the dark passengers on a ship can see it, for at night it is lighted with very strong lights. Travelers returning to America from abroad feel they are really home when they sight *The Statue of Liberty*.

The Statue of Liberty is the biggest bronze statue in all the world. This woman is as tall as a ten-story building. Her hand is sixteen feet long. Her eyes are each two and a half feet wide. Her uplifted right arm is forty-two feet long. Her finger is as long as an elephant is high! If you wanted that woman to wear a ring, the ring would have to be as big as a hoop! If you wanted the woman to wear gloves, the material for the gloves would spread over more room than a tennis court!

Such a woman is *Liberty*. She is sometimes called *Liberty Enlightening the World*. This is because *Liberty* holds a lighted torch in her raised right hand. The torch is so big that people climb a ladder inside the right arm and then walk around the torch as if it were a porch.

Held in *Liberty's* left arm is a tablet. On the tablet are these letters:

JULY IV

MDCCLXXVI

Do you know what they mean? Even if you don't know, I'm not going to tell you, so you have a puzzle to work out.

The Statue of Liberty can be seen from a long way off, but you can't get very close to it unless you take a boat. When you get

Bartholdi, **Statue of Liberty,** New York.

New York Convention and Visitors Bureau

off the boat you walk up some steps to the pedestal. Inside the pedestal you take an elevator and ride up to the top of the pedestal. Then you have to climb stairs to reach the top of the statue. The stairs wind round and round inside the statue like a snail's shell, and the higher you climb, the more you feel like going slowly—also like a snail. As you climb you can see the framework that the statue is built around, made of rods of steel. You can see how the statue is fitted together out of separate pieces of bronze.

When you finally get up inside the head you can look out of windows in *Liberty's* crown.

The man who made the huge statue was a Frenchman named Bartholdi (Bar-tōl'dee). A Frenchman made it as a gift from the people of France to the people of the United States. Bartholdi chose the place for *Liberty* to be put and then went back to France and made a model. The model was used to make the huge bronze pieces of the statue itself. These pieces were brought in a ship to the United States and put together on the island. It was like fitting together a gigantic picture puzzle, for of course each piece of bronze was a different shape.

Auguste Rodin

Suppose you were a sculptor and wanted to make a statue meaning *thought*. *Thought* is an idea. In grammar we would call it an abstract noun. How, then, could a sculptor make as solid a material as bronze or marble represent an abstract idea like *thought*?

Of course a sculptor could make a statue of a person sitting as one sits when thinking. He could label this statue "Thought," but without the label it might just as well be "Sleep" or "Rest" or "Fatigue."

The Greeks solved the problem in their way by imagining a goddess of thought or wisdom and then making a statue of the goddess. The statue would look wise, but still it would be just a likeness of a goddess, not of *thought*. Any thoughtful or wise-looking woman might serve for the model.

Let's try another way. A person who does much thinking is generally able to think easily. Often, if he is a very wise and thoughtful person, you may not see him thinking at all. Probably he would not look as if he were thinking, because he could think so easily. He thinks with his brain and not with his muscles.

But watch a boy who is not very bright at his lessons trying to do an arithmetic problem. He does not think easily. He sticks out his tongue. He twists his legs about his chair. He bends his head to one side. He holds his pencil so tight his fingers hurt. You can see him thinking because it is hard for him to do it.

The Metropolitan Museum of Art, Gift of Thomas F. Ryan, 1910.

Or, instead of the boy, imagine a cave man. His muscles are big and powerful, but his mind is not very well developed. Thinking is difficult for him. But sooner or later he will wonder about his life and what is going to come of it. He begins thinking, wondering, pondering with his simple mind. Why is he here in this world? What happens when he dies? Does he just go out like a dying fire or does part of him live on in some other world that he knows nothing about? Even more than the schoolboy, you can see him thinking. If you saw him you would say, "How hard he is thinking!"

A statue of such a cave man would show *thinking* much better than a goddess of thought or a brilliant thinker. A sculptor who used this idea of showing *thinking* by making a statue of someone *trying* hard to think, was a Frenchman, who died in 1917. His name was Auguste Rodin (Ro-danh). His most famous statue is called *The Thinker*. It isn't *thinking*—but a man thinking—a thinker. It is probably as near as anyone can get to showing *thinking* or *thought*.

The statue is of a brute-like man. It isn't smooth and pretty like Canova's *Mercury*. It is roughly and strongly modeled. This rough modeling helps make the man look more brute-like and unused to thinking. He sits pondering, head in hand, pondering so intensely that even his toes are tightly clutching the ground.

Rodin loved contrasts. Often he carved delicate and beautiful forms as though they were just coming out of the uncarved marble block. The beauty is increased by the contrast of the finished part with the unfinished.

Rodin, **The Thinker.**

Some Early American Sculptors

Lent by the Commissioners of Fairmount Park. Photograph courtesy Philadelphia Museum of Art.

William Rush, **Water Nymph and Bittern** (Nymph of the Schuylkill).

I've told you about sculpture from Egypt and Assyria, Greece and Rome, Italy and France, but nothing about sculpture made in the United States.

The reason I haven't told you about American sculpture is that American sculpture was late in starting. Probably the last thing the early settlers would have thought of bringing across the ocean to America would have been a statue. Statues aren't easy to carry around and the ships were small and crowded. Then when the settlers got to America they were too busy even to try to make statues. They had to chop down trees, build homes, plant crops, fight Indians, explore the country. Two hundred years after the first white settlement of America, they could boast of no real sculptors and, of course, they had no sculpture of their own.

At that time ships were built along the seacoast to hunt whales and to bring back goods from other countries. These were splendid square-rigged sailing vessels. The owners were proud of their ships and decorated the ships' bows—the front part—with wooden figures called *figureheads*. These figureheads were usually the figures of mermaids or sea nymphs and seemed to be sprouting out of the bows of the ships. Some figureheads were full-length figures, some were carved as far as the waist, and some were simply busts. Figureheads were nearly always brightly painted.

William Rush was the best of the figurehead carvers. He was the first real American sculptor. When he was a young man he was a soldier in the American Revolution, and afterward an important citizen of Philadelphia. William Rush made many figureheads, but he carved also a life-size statue of Washington in wood. His best carving in wood is *The Spirit of the Schuylkill* (School'kill) *River*. Rush's friends said that no greater piece of art was to be found in all the world than this statue of the Schuylkill's Spirit. We don't think it is as great as that now, but for a country that hadn't had any sculptors, it was good. Later the Schuylkill statue was cast in bronze and it stands now in Fairmount Park in Philadelphia.

The next important American sculptor was Horatio Greenough. His most famous statue was of George Washington. Greenough worked on it seven years in Italy. It is now in Washington, D.C. Washington, in this statue, is dressed only in a kind of sheet, just as if he were a Greek god. Zeus was the head of the Greek gods and Washington was the head of the United States, so Greenough carved this statue with the body of Zeus and the head of Washington. It looks very strange to us now. It was made in marble and is larger than life-size.

Born the same year as Horatio Greenough was Hiram Powers. Hiram Powers carved a statue in marble that for many years was the most famous statue by an American. It was a marble statue called *The Greek Slave*. It is a young woman with her hands bound together by a heavy chain. Powers carved *The Greek Slave* in Italy because good marble hadn't been discovered in America.

Then came a sculptor named Thomas Crawford. He was given the job of making figures for the pediment, or triangular space, made by the sloping roof at one end of the Capitol that was being built in Washington. Crawford called the figures that he made for this pediment, *The Past and Present of the Republic*. If you ever visit Washington, D.C., be sure to look at Crawford's statues. They are on the Senate end of the Capitol.

Also in Washington, on the very top of the dome of the Capitol, is a statue that from the ground looks like an Indian. Many people think it is supposed to be an Indian. Really it is a statue of *Liberty*. It also was done by Thomas Crawford.

Many sculptors have done work for the Capitol at Washington. Another of these sculptors was Randolph Rogers. You remember the *Gates of Paradise* by Ghiberti. Randolph Rogers made two bronze doors for the Capitol that remind us of Ghiberti's doors for the Baptistery. There are eight small pictures in relief showing the life of Columbus. One of the reliefs shows Columbus with his hand out in front of him. The hand is just the right height to reach easily, so visitors to the Capitol always take hold of it. Then when they go home they can say, "I shook hands with Columbus." So many people have shaken hands with Columbus that the hand has become worn and shiny. Someday the hand will be worn away altogether! The Rogers doors were cast in bronze in Europe. The European bronze casters would not tell American sculptors how to cast in bronze, so Americans had to find out for themselves. A sculptor named Clark Mills was asked by the Congress of the United States to make a statue of General Andrew Jackson.

Historical Pictures Service, Chicago

Hiram Powers, **The Greek Slave.** Corcoran Gallery of Art, Washington, D.C.

Historical Pictures Service, Chicago

Thomas Crawford, **Liberty,**
sculpture on Capitol Dome,
Washington, D.C.

Historical Pictures Service, Chicago

Randolph Rogers, **Bronze Doors** of central east entrance,
Capitol Building, Washington, D.C.

General Jackson had recently died. He had been a famous
fighter and twice President of the United States.

Making this statue was going to be a tough job for Clark
Mills. The statue was to be in bronze, and no bronze statue had
ever been cast in the United States. What's more, no equestrian
statue had ever been made in the United States. What's more,
the sculptor Mills had never seen an equestrian statue. What's
more, Mills had never seen General Jackson! But, in spite of all
these things against him, Clark Mills went to work. He got
bronze by melting bronze cannon that General Jackson had
captured.

Campbell Photo Service, Washington, D.C.

Clark Mills, **Andrew Jackson,** Washington, D.C.

Art Commission of the City of New York   American Airlines

Finally the statue was completed and set up in Washington. It showed General Jackson taking off his hat as if he were acknowledging the cheers of a crowd. The horse is rearing back on its hind legs. You remember that *The Gattamelata* statue has a ball under the horse's front foot. The *Andrew Jackson* statue has both front feet of the horse off the ground, but it is well balanced just on the two back feet. The United States Congress liked the statue so much that they gave the sculptor twenty thousand dollars extra, and the city of New Orleans had one just like it set up there.

The Mills statue of Jackson isn't considered as fine a piece of sculpture now as it was when it was new—just like Powers' *Greek Slave* and Rush's wooden *Spirit of the Schuylkill*. But don't forget how hard it was to make this first American equestrian statue.

There was an early American sculptor whose work is still thought to be among the best. He was named for a President— John Quincy Adams Ward. Ward made a statue called *Indian Hunter* that stands in Central Park, New York City. The Indian has a bow and arrow in one hand and is holding back his dog with the other.

Ward's best statue is *George Washington*. The statue stands on the steps at the entrance of the Sub-Treasury building in New York City. It looks something like Houdon's *Washington at Richmond*, but it is better than Houdon's.

opposite left: John Quincy Adams Ward, **Indian Hunter.** Central Park, New York.

---

opposite right: John Quincy Adams Ward, **George Washington,** New York.

Augustus Saint-Gaudens

Now I'm going to tell you about Saint-Gaudens. Saint-Gaudens wasn't a Christian martyr, like Saint George; Saint-Gaudens didn't preach sermons to birds, as Saint Francis did; Saint-Gaudens wasn't one of the Apostles, like Saint John. In fact, Saint-Gaudens wasn't a saint at all. His last name was Saint-Gaudens just as it might have been Adams or Von Hindenburg. His first name was Augustus.

Augustus Saint-Gaudens was a fine man, and a very fine sculptor. What a fine sculptor!

There is one way we know he was a truly great sculptor—his work is liked by many different kinds of people. Young people and adults, rich people and poor people, stupid people and wise people—all praise the statues that Augustus Saint-Gaudens made.

Saint-Gaudens' first great statue was of Admiral Farragut. Admiral Farragut was an officer in the United States Navy during the American Civil War. The statue, which stands in Madison Square, in New York City, shows the admiral as he must have looked standing on the deck of his ship. His feet are apart to brace him to the roll of the ship on the sea. His coat is blown back by the wind. His cap is pulled tight on his head on account of the stiff sea breeze. His face is strong and he looks determined, as if he had made up his mind to win no matter what happened.

Look at the base or pedestal on which the statue stands. Most pedestals are just big blocks of stone to hold the statue high. But *Admiral Farragut's* pedestal is really part of the statue. An architect—a man who designs buildings—helped Saint-Gaudens design the pedestal. Look at the streaks that make you think of sea water. Notice the dolphins at the ends. Notice the naval sword that carries your eye up again to the admiral.

Art Commission of the City of New York

Augustus Saint-Gaudens, **Admiral Farragut.** Madison Square, New York.

THE GIFT OF ELI BATES

Chicago Park District

Notice one other thing: Admiral Farragut is in his uniform and the uniform has trousers. This is the first statue I've shown you that shows trousers. Sculptors made their bronze or marble men in knee breeches in George Washington's time. When men began to wear long trousers, the sculptors had a hard time. Trousers in statues are apt to look like stovepipes or logs instead of like cloth leg coverings. Sculptors still think that men's clothes with trousers are not very suitable for statues. But Saint-Gaudens didn't let that spoil his statues. His statues are good even in trousers.

Saint-Gaudens's *Lincoln* is one of the best-loved statues in America. It stands in Lincoln Park in the city of Chicago. A copy of it was given to Great Britain by the United States and was put up near Westminster Abbey in London. Lincoln stands before a chair of state, or a president's chair. He looks as if he had just stood up to say something to the people before him. Lincoln's face seems very serious. It is a face that has in it both strength and gentleness. Saint-Gaudens's *Abraham Lincoln* has dignity and simplicity.

The *Farragut* and *Lincoln* statues are of leaders in the Civil War. So is the next statue in this book. Saint-Gaudens was much too young at the time to be in the Civil War himself. But after the war, people wanted statues of the war heroes and Saint-Gaudens was chosen to make some of them.

Saint-Gaudens made a statue in memory of a Civil War officer, Colonel Shaw, who commanded the first Negro regiment from Massachusetts. The statue stands in Boston, on the spot from which Colonel Shaw and his soldiers started out for the war.

Augustus Saint-Gaudens, **Abraham Lincoln.** Lincoln Park, Chicago.

Shaw Commercial Photo Service, Boston

The Shaw Memorial is in relief. It shows the young colonel mounted on a horse and riding beside the marching Negroes of his regiment. Above in the sky flies the Angel of Death. Saint-Gaudens put the Angel of Death there because Colonel Shaw was killed in battle with many of his soldiers, a few months after marching out of Boston.

The sculptor worked on this relief for fourteen years. Again and again he made changes until he felt that every part of the statue was right. In fact, he was so careful to make it a good memorial that he spent more money making it than he was paid for doing it. The marching soldiers, the slanting rifles, the spirited horse, the forward look of the rider, the drawn sword, give such swing and life to the whole statue that you can almost hear the tramp of the feet and the beat of the drums.

Do you remember the equestrian statue that is called the best in all the world? And the equestrian statue called the next-best in all the world? Now we come to the equestrian statue that has been called the third-best equestrian statue. The sculptor was Saint-Gaudens. The statue is *General Sherman*. General Sherman was a Northern leader in the war between the North and the South. The statue shows General Sherman riding forward behind the Angel of Victory.

The *Sherman* statue is made of bronze, but it is painted with gold paint or gilt so that it isn't the same color as other bronze statues. It stands in the Plaza in New York City and everyone riding uptown or downtown on a Fifth Avenue bus can see it close at hand. It was done by the man who is called the best American sculptor of all.

left: Augustus Saint-Gaudens, **The Shaw Memorial,** Boston.

right: Augustus Saint-Gaudens, **General Sherman,** New York.

Art Commission of the City of New York

Daniel Chester French

The Great Sphinx is the biggest stone statue in the world. *The Statue of Liberty* is the biggest bronze statue in the world. The biggest marble statue in the world is in the Lincoln Memorial in Washington. The Lincoln Memorial is a beautiful marble building given by the United States in memory of President Lincoln. The statue inside is a huge figure of Abraham Lincoln. It is made up of twenty large pieces of marble so carefully carved and fitted together that the statue seems to be all one piece.

Now, just because a statue is big doesn't mean that it is beautiful. A little piece of sculpture as big as your hand may be much more beautiful than a huge statue as big as a house. But this biggest marble statue *is* beautiful. It is great in other ways than just bigness.

The Lincoln statue is the only one in the building. Do you remember the Parthenon, another great shrine with a single statue inside? The inner walls of the Lincoln Memorial are decorated with huge paintings, but the whole building seems made just to hold this one statue. Lincoln is seated in a peculiar kind of chair that looks like a throne. He sits facing the door so that you stand before him when you enter.

The whole memorial is so beautiful and impressive, so simple and so fitting, that you feel as if the spirit of Lincoln were in the building.

The sculptor of this wonderful *Abraham Lincoln* was Daniel Chester French. Let me tell you about two of his many other statues.

Daniel Chester French, **Abraham Lincoln,** The Lincoln Memorial, Washington, D.C.

American Airlines

Daniel Chester French carved *The Minute Man* that stands on the battlefield at Concord, Massachusetts. Where the statue stands, the road crosses a little wooden bridge over a stream and it was at this crossing that the New England farmers fired on the British soldiers—fired "the shot heard round the world." *The Minute Man* was placed there in memory of those farmer soldiers. They were called minute men because they kept themselves ready to go to fight the enemy at a minute's notice. The statue shows a Minute Man who is plowing when the call to arms comes. He leaves the plow in the field as he snatches his musket. It was French's first statue, made when he was twenty-three.

Some years later Daniel Chester French made a statue called *Death Staying the Hand of the Sculptor*. The statue shows the Angel of Death reaching out her hand to take the hand of a young sculptor who is carving a sphinx in bas relief. Of course when Death takes his hand the sculptor must leave his work unfinished. The statue is in memory of a young sculptor named Millmore, who died almost at the beginning of his work. It is sometimes called *The Millmore Memorial*.

Historical Pictures Service, Chicago

above: Daniel Chester French, **The Minute Man.** Concord, Massachusetts.

right: Daniel Chester French, **Death Staying the Hand of the Sculptor, (Martin Millmore Memorial).** Forest Hills Cemetery, Boston.

Historical Pictures Service, Chicago

Women Sculptors
in America

Men have made so many good statues that there isn't room in one book to tell you about them all. Perhaps you notice that I said *men* have made so many good statues. What about women? It is true that all the statues that I have told you about so far have been made by men. Until recently women have not been good sculptors. They have not often been sculptors at all—until recently.

The first person to make portrait statues in America was a woman whose name is now unimportant. Her portrait statues were very lifelike. They were made of wax and colored to look like real people and were just the same size as real people. She even dressed them in real clothes just like the wax figures in a clothing store. And then later Madame Tussaud made the same kind of wax figures of people famous in history. Madame Tussaud's Waxworks are in London and there you can see such men as Napoleon and Theodore Roosevelt and Marshal Foch all looking so lifelike that they really seem ready to speak.

But waxworks aren't considered real sculpture, any more than a colored photograph is considered a real painting. After the early waxworks more and more women studied to be sculptors, especially in the United States, until now there are women sculptors who are just as good as men sculptors and so many of them that I can't begin to tell you about all of them. There is room here for only two, I'm sorry to say.

One of these two is Mrs. Anna Hyatt Huntington. Mrs. Huntington had two favorite subjects for her statues. She is famous for her animal statues and for her Joan of Arc statues. The statue pictured combines both subjects. It is of Joan of Arc on a horse. Some people who write about art (art critics) say that this statue of Joan of Arc is the best Joan of Arc statue that anyone has ever made.

Art Commission of the City of New York

Anna Hyatt Huntington, **Joan of Arc,** New York.

Most statues of Joan of Arc show her as too old or too big or too adult looking. Joan of Arc was only seventeen when she led the French armies against their enemies. In Mrs. Huntington's statue Joan looks only seventeen. Then again, people who know about the kind of armor worn in the time of Joan of Arc say that Mrs. Huntington is the first sculptor to put exactly the right armor and equipment on Joan and on Joan's horse.

Perhaps you think the horse is too big for Joan. But probably it's more nearly the kind of horse the real Joan rode than a smaller one would be. I told you warhorses had to be big and strong to carry the men in armor and to charge through the enemy. It's very likely that when Joan took command of the army she was given a man's warhorse to ride. Before fire engines became automobiles they used to be pulled by large and beautiful horses. The horse that Mrs. Huntington used as a model for her statue was a fire engine horse in Gloucester, Massachusetts.

The Huntington *Joan of Arc* stands on Riverside Drive in New York City. Do you like it as well as Frémiet's *Joan of Arc*? I like it better.

The other woman sculptor I want you to know is Gertrude Vanderbilt Whitney. Mrs. Whitney won the competition for a monument in memory of the people who were drowned when the *Titanic* sank. The *Titanic* was a great new ocean liner. On her first trip across the Atlantic she ran upon an iceberg and tore a hole in her bottom. She sank before other ships could reach her and more than fifteen hundred people were lost. The memorial designed by Mrs. Whitney shows a human figure standing erect with arms outstretched like a cross. It was made to be placed in Washington, D.C.

And now for Buffalo Bill, the daring Western scout. He has an equestrian statue in his honor. Buffalo Bill's real name was William Cody, Colonel William Cody later, and the statue of Buffalo Bill stands in the little town of Cody, Wyoming, which Buffalo Bill founded. The statue, made by Mrs. Whitney, shows Buffalo Bill looking down into a valley signaling with his rifle to the wagon train that he is guiding through the Indian country. The horse in the statue was modeled from one of Buffalo Bill's own horses.

Though I've mentioned only two women sculptors, there are many more women who are making excellent statues.

Historical Pictures Service, Chicago

Gertrude Vanderbilt Whitney,
The Titanic Memorial.

Gertrude Vanderbilt Whitney, **Buffalo Bill.** Cody, Wyoming.

Buffalo Bill Historical Center, Cody, Wyoming

Modern Sculpture

Modern sculpture can be nonrealistic just as painting can. Nonrealistic sculpture gives the idea, the thought, the impression of something. The sculptor doesn't try to make an exact copy of something he sees.

If you will look at the sculpture called *Bird in Space* you will see an example of nonrealistic sculpture. You can see that it doesn't look like a bird. But it does give the idea of flight. The flight of a bird depends on wings and this sculpture seems to be all wing. At least most people think it looks winglike. It is a smooth streamlined wing shape. Constantin Brancusi, its sculptor, carved no feathers, no body, no head or tail of a bird. Some people think that a piece of sculpture called a bird should look like a bird. In this sculpture, however, the flight of a bird, not the bird itself, is the important idea.

Nonrealistic sculpture is a twentieth century kind of sculpture. Brancusi was one of the first to develop this style. He was born in Romania and studied art there as a young man. Then he went to Paris and worked in the studio of the great French sculptor Auguste Rodin. At first his sculpture was realistic, like Rodin's. But he became interested in nonrealistic sculpture and soon stopped making realistic statues.

Brancusi not only made new forms of sculpture but he tried using many different materials. He made sculptures in wood, bronze, marble, stone, glass, and steel. *Bird in Space* is his best-known work.

The sculpture called *Girl Washing Her Hair* is by Hugo Robus, an American born in Cleveland. It is much more realistic than Brancusi's *Bird in Space*. It isn't, however, very realistic. It isn't a portrait. It has no eyes, nose, or mouth to show which girl this is. It's any girl. What she is doing is more important than who she is. The sculptor didn't need to show us a whole person to let us see that hairwashing is being done. If anything else were added (like a nose or mouth or feet) it would not make the idea of hairwashing any clearer.

It's fun to find a piece of sculpture that is not too dignified and serious. Most sculpture has been, in the past, very dignified and very serious. There are the busts of powerful men like the Roman emperors, statues of Greek gods and of heroes on horse-

Philadelphia Museum of Art, Louise and Walter Arensberg Collection. Photograph by A. J. Wyatt, Staff Photographer.

Constantin Brancusi,
Bird in Space.

Courtesy of The Art Institute of Chicago. Gift of Florene May Schoenborn and Samuel A. Marx.

Courtesy of The Art Institute of Chicago. Gift of Mr. and Mrs. R. Howard Goldsmith.

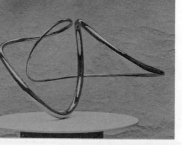

top: Isamu Noguchi,
Man Walking.

---

bottom: José de Rivera,
Brussels Construction.

back and of Christian saints. There are imaginary figures called Victory, or Liberty, or Justice. These are all very solemn and impressive statues, as if the sculptors didn't want to waste their valuable time and marble on unimportant subjects that are familiar and amusing.

People, however, like familiar and amusing things. Statues of the kind of people we see every day, doing the things we all do, are usually well liked. More and more modern sculptors are carving these familiar and everyday kind of people like the *Girl Washing Her Hair.* Nobody ever saw Victory or Liberty or Justice washing their hair, even as statues.

Remember the statue called *Boy with Thorn.* Even two thousand years ago some sculptors had found it fun to make such familiar, everyday, amusing statues. *Boy with Thorn* is much more realistic than *Girl Washing Her Hair.*

You don't have to go to a museum to see the different kinds of sculpture. Every city has sculptures in parks and on monuments and on the outside of buildings.

In Washington, D.C., there is sculpture almost everywhere. In New York City, at Rockefeller Center there is a large bronze piece of sculpture called *Prometheus.* It is by a famous American sculptor, Paul Manship. And at the New York Zoological Park there are beautiful bronze entrance gates. They are also by Paul Manship. Entrance gates to a zoo, you might think, should be decorated with carvings of animals. Paul Manship thought so too. The bronze work around the gates is full of wild animals: bears, deer, baboons, lions. Paul Manship's work is realistic and has a fine decorative quality.

A Swedish-American sculptor, Carl Milles, designed Millesgarden, a park near Stockholm, Sweden, on an island called Ludingo. The park provides a beautiful setting for this sculptor's works. Milles made many heroic-size monuments and is especially well known for his fountain designs. Many of his monumental figures have an amusing twist, such as the sculptured angel who wears a wristwatch!

Modern sculpture, you see, is of several kinds. Some is nonrealistic like Brancusi's *Bird in Space.* Some is more realistic, giving the general form of an object but not trying to be a close copy of the living thing, like *Girl Washing Her Hair* by Robus. And some modern sculpture is realistic, but decorative, like Paul Manship's *Prometheus* and his animals of the zoological gates. All three kinds of modern sculpture are worth seeing.

New York Zoological Society Photo

above: Paul Manship, **Paul J. Rainey Memorial Gate,**
The New York Zoological Park (Bronx Zoo).

right: Carl Milles, **Poseidon,** Malmo.

below: Carl Milles, **Millesgården.**

The Royal Consulate General of Sweden in Chicago

The Royal Consulate General of Sweden in Chicago

The End of the Trail

Do you save the best things till last? Well, I've saved until last several statues that I think you may like best of all. They are not supposed to be quite as great and famous as the Greek sculpture, or the best Renaissance statues, or Saint-Gaudens's work, but here they are.

The first of these statues is a monument in memory of Eugene Field. Eugene Field was the man who wrote "Wynken, Blynken, and Nod," and "The Sugar Plum Tree." The sculptor might have made a portrait bust of Eugene Field, but instead he made something much more interesting. It is a statue of a little boy and girl who have fallen sound asleep because a fairy has waved poppy blossoms over them. Poppy blossoms, you know, are supposed to make you sleepy. You can see the poppy blossoms in the fairy's hand.

The fairy and the little boy and girl are in full round. Then there are scenes carved in low relief. One scene shows Wynken, Blynken, and Nod sailing along in the wooden shoe, with fish jumping all around them. You remember in the song they had nets of silver and gold. You can see the nets hanging from the stern of the shoe. Another scene shows the Sugar Plum Tree with a cat up in the branches and a little dog and some children looking up at the cat.

The sculptor who made the *Eugene Field Memorial* (it is really a fountain in Chicago) is Edward McCartan of New York. He also made a very beautiful marble statue of the moon goddess, Diana, out hunting with her greyhound.

The next sculptor is Alexander Phimister Proctor, who has made statues of cowboys, Indians, and animals. He helped Saint-Gaudens model the horse for the *Sherman* statue. Proctor's best-known works are the famous *Princeton Tigers*. There are two big bronze tigers, one on each side of the entrance to Nassau Hall, a building at Princeton University.

opposite top: Edward McCartan, **Eugene Field Memorial**, Lincoln Park, Chicago.

opposite bottom: Alexander Phimister Proctor, **The Princeton Tigers**, Princeton, New Jersey.

Princeton University

Chicago Park District

Santa Fe Railway Photo

Now look at the *Bronco Buster* by the same sculptor. It stands in Denver, Colorado. The bronco, or cowboy horse, is trying to throw its rider. The bronco has bucked high in the air and is coming down stiff-legged on its two front feet. What a jolt the cowboy must be getting! Notice how the whole weight of this equestrian statue is carried by the two front legs of the horse.

James Earle Fraser is the sculptor we have saved until the very last. We can call him an all-round sculptor because he is good at large statues in the round as well as reliefs and portraits, medals and coins. He can do people and animals. He has modeled for equestrian statues horses that are more than life-size and he made the tiny buffalo on the old United States five-cent coin—the buffalo nickel. He did a statue of Alexander Hamilton. It is a wonderful statue, full of dignity and grace.

James Earle Fraser designed the Victory Medal given to each American who served in the army or navy during World War I. Perhaps someone in your family has one of these medals. The medal has on the front side a bas relief figure of Victory. As this is an American medal, the sculptor put a crown with spikes on Victory's head like the crown on *The Statue of Liberty*. On the back are the names of the countries who fought with America in the war, and a United States shield.

Fraser made a wonderful portrait bust of President Theodore Roosevelt, who liked it so much he said he would never pose for another bust.

Campbell Photo Service, Washington, D.C.

left: Alexander Phimister Proctor, **Bronco Buster,** Denver.

---

right: James Earle Fraser, **Alexander Hamilton.**

And now last of all comes Fraser's best-known statue. It is the famous *End of the Trail*—an exhausted Indian on a weary, worn-out horse. A strong wind blows at their backs. You can see the Indian's blanket and the horse's tail whipped forward by this wind. Everything suggests weariness. The horse's head droops low, the Indian's nods forward, his spear points to the ground. You feel that both horse and rider have made a terrible journey, without rest, and have reached the end of the trail too tired to keep awake any longer. *The End of the Trail* is to mark in San Francisco, California, the western end of the auto highway that runs across the United States from the Atlantic to the Pacific.

In this book it will mark the end of our trail of sculpture. And now that our trip along the trail of sculpture is finished, from ancient Egypt to modern America, I hope you are not as tired out at the end of the trail as Fraser's Indian seems to be. Our trip had to be short, so we missed seeing some of the finest statues and talking about some very good sculptors. And that is really a good thing. There is so much left for you to see that it should make you want to take the sculpture trail again and learn to know the sculpture that hasn't been mentioned in this book. You, like Buffalo Bill, will have to search for signs along the trail. I wish you a very happy journey.

James Earle Fraser, **End of the Trail**, San Francisco.

INDEX: *Young People's Story of Sculpture*

Type   Century Expanded
Typesetter   American Typesetting Corporation
Printer   The Regensteiner Corporation